Celine Dion

Celine Dion

Titles in the People in the News series include:

PEOPLE
IN THE **NEWS**

Celine Dion

by Joanne Mattern

LUCENT BOOKS
SAN DIEGO, CALIFORNIA

THOMSON
━━━✶━━━ ™
GALE

Detroit • New York • San Diego • San Francisco
Boston • New Haven, Conn. • Waterville, Maine
London • Munich

Library of Congress Cataloging-in-Publication Data

Mattern, Joanne. 1963–
    Celine Dion / by Joanne Mattern.
        p. cm. — (People in the news)
    Includes bibliographical references (p.   ) and index.
        ISBN 1-59018-137-9
    1. Dion, Câeline—Juvenile literature. 2. Singers—Canada—
Biography—Juvenile literature. [1. Dion,
Câeline. 2. Singers. 3. Women—Biography.] I. Title. II. People in the
news (San Diego, Calif.)
ML3930.D47 M38 2002
782.42164'092—dc21

2001006216

Copyright © 2002 by Lucent Books,
an imprint of The Gale Group
10911 Technology Place, San Diego, CA 92127
Printed in the U.S.A.

Table of Contents

Foreword

FAME AND CELEBRITY are alluring. People are drawn to those who walk in fame's spotlight, whether they are known for great accomplishments or for notorious deeds. The lives of the famous pique public interest and attract attention, perhaps because their experiences seem in some ways so different from, yet in other ways so similar to, our own.

Newspapers, magazines, and television regularly capitalize on this fascination with celebrity by running profiles of famous people. For example, television programs such as *Entertainment Tonight* devote all of their programming to stories about entertainment and entertainers. Magazines such as *People* fill their pages with stories of the private lives of famous people. Even newspapers, newsmagazines, and television news frequently delve into the lives of well-known personalities. Despite the number of articles and programs, few provide more than a superficial glimpse at their subjects.

Lucent's People in the News series offers young readers a deeper look into the lives of today's newsmakers, the influences that have shaped them, and the impact they have had in their fields of endeavor and on other people's lives. The subjects of the series hail from many disciplines and walks of life. They include authors, musicians, athletes, political leaders, entertainers, entrepreneurs, and others who have made a mark on modern life and who, in many cases, will continue to do so for years to come.

These biographies are more than factual chronicles. Each book emphasizes the contributions, accomplishments, or deeds that have brought fame or notoriety to the individual and shows how that person has influenced modern life. Authors portray their subjects in a realistic, unsentimental light. For example, Bill Gates—the cofounder and chief executive officer of the software giant Microsoft—has been instrumental in making personal computers the most vital tool of the modern age. Few dispute his business savvy, his perseverance, or his technical expertise, yet critics say he is ruthless in his dealings with competitors and driven more by his desire to maintain Microsoft's dominance in the computer industry than by an interest in furthering technology.

In these books, young readers will encounter inspiring stories about real people who achieved success despite enormous obstacles. Oprah Winfrey—the most powerful, most watched, and wealthiest woman on television today—spent the first six years of her life in the care of her grandparents while her unwed mother sought work and a better life elsewhere. Her adolescence was colored by promiscuity, pregnancy at age fourteen, rape, and sexual abuse.

Each author documents and supports his or her work with an array of primary and secondary source quotations taken from diaries, letters, speeches, and interviews. All quotes are footnoted to show readers exactly how and where biographers derive their information and provide guidance for further research. The quotations enliven the text by giving readers eyewitness views of the life and accomplishments of each person covered in the People in the News series.

In addition, each book in the series includes photographs, annotated bibliographies, timelines, and comprehensive indexes. For both the casual reader and the student researcher, the People in the News series offers insight into the lives of today's newsmakers—people who shape the way we live, work, and play in the modern age.

A Charmed Life

H ER CDS HAVE sold millions of copies all over the world. Her music has touched the lives of countless people. Her own life includes a love story that could be right out of a fairy tale. Her name is Celine Dion.

Celine Dion burst out of a small town in Canada to become one of the most successful and compelling stars in music history. She has sold more than 100 million CDs in the past ten years. Many journalists and music historians call her the top female pop vocalist of all time.

Dreams and Determination

Dion has had many dreams come true in her life. She has always said there are two reasons for her incredible success: her family and her own determination to succeed. As the youngest child of a large French-Canadian family, she learned to love music and performing from an early age. As she grew older, her family stood behind her dream of becoming a successful singer. Dion's mother and brother even wrote a special song for Dion—a song that attracted the attention of Canada's top music manager, René Angelil.

Angelil became an important part of Dion's life, both professionally and personally. He guided Dion's career from the time she was twelve years old and accompanied her on tours and appearances around the world. He was more than her manager—he was her mentor and her friend. In time, despite the age difference between Dion and her manager, the two fell in love. Eventually, they married and started a family.

The support of Angelil and her family was a big part of Dion's career. But the biggest reason for her success was Dion's determination. Throughout her life, she has made entertaining her number one priority. Her incredible hard work, combined with a powerful voice, have guided her to the top of the entertainment world.

Dion has led a charmed life. However, like everyone, she has suffered setbacks and losses in both her professional and personal lives. Serious illness, a heartbreaking romance, and career-threatening vocal damage have all challenged this remarkable woman. Dion's life is not just interesting to read about, it is an amazing example of how dedication and love can lead to success.

Chapter 1

A Musical Childhood

Celine Dion's love of music can be traced directly back to her childhood. As the youngest member of a close-knit and very talented family, she was surrounded by music from the day she was born. In fact, her family—which was unusual, even in the history of show business—provided the foundation for Dion's career and helped her reach her dreams.

A Traditional Marriage, an Unconventional Family

Celine Dion was born on March 30, 1968, in Charlemagne, a small town nine miles north of Montreal in Quebec, Canada. Charlemagne is a working-class town where almost everyone speaks French. Celine herself would not begin to learn English until her late teenage years.

Dion's parents, Adhemar and Thérèse Dion, were hardworking French Canadians. Adhemar worked eighteen-hour days in a factory to support his large family, while Thérèse took care of the house and the children. It was a traditional marriage, but the family was far from conventional!

At first, Adhemar, Thérèse, and their growing family lived in a crowded, run-down apartment. Every day, Adhemar walked to work to save forty cents on bus fare. After a few years, the family was able to save enough money to buy some land in Charlemagne. But they had no money to hire workers to build a house. So they built it themselves.

Adhemar would work all day at the factory, then stay up all night working on the house. Thérèse soon had all the neighbors talking as they watched her climb ladders and hammer nails into the roof. The neighbors were shocked because Thérèse was pregnant with her seventh child at the time. "Never once did my mother let her pregnancies get in the way of her responsibilities or the needs of her family,"[1] Celine said proudly.

Before becoming pregnant with Celine, who would be her fourteenth child, Thérèse was sure her childbearing days were over. The youngest of her children, six-year-old twins Paul and Pauline, were in school, and at forty-one, Thérèse looked forward to leaving the house, getting a job, and traveling. Her pregnancy with Celine changed all that.

A Surprise Arrival

In her autobiography, *My Story, My Dream,* Dion admits that "I was a mistake, an accident, and the cause of a serious quandary for my

Celine Dion's parents, Adhemar and Thérèse Dion. Celine was their fourteenth child.

mother. The day she learned she was pregnant, she had to relinquish plans she'd been cherishing a long time. I was in no way a part of these plans. My birth was unwanted and unexpected. By coming into the world, I crushed her dreams. I've always loved her so much that if I had known this, I think I would not have been able to let myself be born."[2]

Despite her mother's initial misgivings, Celine Dion was warmly welcomed into the family. She was named for a song that was popular in Quebec at the time, "Dis-Moi Celine" ("Call Me Celine") by Hugues Aufray. Dion's eight sisters and five brothers, who ranged in age from six to twenty-two, overwhelmed the new baby with love and attention. "I spent the first days, weeks, or maybe months of my life in the arms of my mother or father, or one of my 13 older brothers and sisters," Dion recalled in her autobiography. "I was the focus of interest for these 15 people, without a doubt the most attentive and indulgent audience I've ever had. They watched me, pampered me, worshiped me. In the evening they argued about whose bed I'd sleep in."[3]

Dion delighted in her close family. "There was love, music, the smell of food, affection,"[4] she told an interviewer years later. For her, home was the very best place to be.

A Musical Family

Like many Canadian families, the Dions loved music. Canadian singer Rita McNeil has said, "Music is a big part of Canada. There's not a home where no one plays an instrument, and there's a lot of heritage from Scottish traditions, French culture, and native Indians, so it's unique."[5] Dion's parents had actually met through music. When Thérèse was eighteen, she played a Quebec folk song called "Le reel de Sainte Anne" ("The Reel of Saint Anne") on her violin at a community dance in her hometown of La Tuque. Twenty-two-year-old Adhemar got up to join her, playing his accordion. Ten months later, the music-loving couple was married.

Dion's father and mother continued to play music after they were married. Dion's brothers and sisters also played instruments and enjoyed singing. Dion recalled how her childhood was rich in music and love:

> I had the incredible luck to be born into a home that was filled with music and song from morning until night—sometimes even from evening until morning. The music of others . . . as well as our own music. The music that my parents played—my father with his accordion and my mother with her violin—reels, gigs, the lively dance music called rigadoons. And the music that my brothers and sisters played with their guitars, pianos, percussion instruments. . . . We were far from rich. But we loved each other. And we had our music, which in addition to health and love, represents

Dion grew up in a musical family.

what's most beautiful and precious in this world. I really believe that where there is music, happiness can't be far behind.[6]

Almost every night, the Dion family made music. "You couldn't hear yourself think in the house, because there were several kinds of music playing at the same time." Describing the activities of her sisters and brothers, Dion writes:

> Ghislaine and Claudette would be singing upstairs in the girls' big bedroom. Down below, Jacques would be playing the guitar, Clement the drums, Daniel the piano. . . . But most often, someone, my father or my mother, imposed some order on the chaos and everybody ended up making music together. This could last hours, all evening, if not through part of the night.[7]

Even mealtimes were an occasion to make music together. The family tapped knives and forks on their glasses to play songs. Since each glass held a different amount of liquid, it produced a different note. Dion also enjoyed watching her sisters imitate performers as they sang along to songs on the radio. Soon Dion was doing the same thing. When she was about two and a half years old, her sisters began dressing her up and putting makeup on her face. Then Dion would perform using the kitchen table for a stage and a fork or spoon as a microphone.

Singing in Public

Dion made her public singing debut in 1973, when she was just five years old. The occasion was her brother Michel's wedding. Dion recalls the day vividly in her autobiography:

> I'll never forget the day I sang in public for the first time. . . . My brothers and sisters had put together a real show for the newlyweds. They set up an entire stage, complete with lighting and amplifiers. We began by singing folk songs together, then each of us did his or her own little number. . . . When it was my turn to go onstage, I became paralyzed by stage fright. Everyone was watching me and waiting for me to begin. These people intimidated me: cousins I'd hardly ever seen, friends of my brothers and sisters who probably knew nothing about music and didn't want to hear me perform. . . . Then I felt my mother's hand on my back, pushing me gently and firmly. And her voice was saying to me: "Go ahead, my little girl, go ahead, it's your turn." So I stepped forward and sang. I don't remember exactly what happened after this, but I do remember not wanting to stop and begging Michel to let me sing other songs. I also sang in all the groups formed by my brothers and sisters. That day gave me great pleasure, a feeling of having conquered my fear, my stage fright. And I definitely knew for the first time in my life that unforgettable sensation felt by a singer when she realizes that she's captivated a listener, that she's being heard, applauded. That day I knew I would be singing my whole life. And that I'd discover my happiness in doing so.[8]

An image of Dion as a child is projected behind her as she performs on stage.

Dion's family was equally captivated by the young performer. "It was at that point we realized she would become a famous singer,"[9] her older sister Claudette said.

Le Vieux Baril

Dion's family loved music so much, they decided to make a living from it. At first, the parents and older children formed a musical group, A. Dion and His Ensemble, that performed at weddings and parties in eastern Quebec. But they wanted to do more.

In 1978, Adhemar and Thérèse bought a restaurant and piano bar called Le Vieux Baril (The Old Barrel), which featured local performers. Owning the restaurant allowed the Dions to share their love of music with the community while earning money. Dion spent hours at the restaurant, even when she was very young. She recalls how her parents would find her "at four in the morning, sleeping on a bench."[10]

Dion also performed at Le Vieux Baril. By the time she was ten years old, Dion was a confident entertainer and a favorite with local audiences. People even called the restaurant or stopped Thérèse or Adhemar in the street to find out what time the youngest Dion would be performing.

Dion's parents enjoyed their daughter's talent and the audiences' positive reaction to her voice. However, they sometimes worried if it was good for such a young child to stay up so late and perform at a bar. However, they soon realized that singing was all that Dion wanted to do. "I had to let her go to the bar and sing or else she would cry,"[11] Dion's mother recalled years later.

Lost in the World

Even though she was close to all of her family, Dion had a special relationship with her mother. The two were rarely apart and, when they were separated, Dion was devastated. "If I slept at the house of one of my married sisters, where my mother sometimes left me for two or three days, I'd always make a big scene," she recalled in *My Story, My Dream*. "I wanted to stay near her all the time, no matter where she was or what she was doing. I think she basically got used to it. Until I was eighteen or nineteen, we were practically inseparable."[12]

Dion was especially upset when she had to leave her mother to go to school. Along with the sorrow of having to spend hours every day apart from her mother and other family members, Dion simply had no interest in making friends with other students. She later wrote:

Close Musical Ties

Celine Dion is not the only member of her family to make a career in the music business. Her brother Michel helps coordinate Dion's tours, and her brother Jacques is a composer. Dion's sister Claudette is a singer and chief hostess at Dion's Nickels restaurant in Repentigny, Quebec. Several of Dion's other siblings, including brothers Clement and Daniel and sisters Pauline, Ghislaine, and Manon, also pursue music as a career or as a hobby, although they do not work for Dion directly.

Dion's family is also an important part of Nickels, a chain of fifties-style restaurants in Canada, which Dion and Angelil created in the 1990s. Her mother owns one restaurant, and her brother Paul owns another, which is managed by Dion's sister Linda.

For me, it wasn't fear of a hostile or strange world, but rather a feeling of boredom. A profound sense of boredom, an immense sadness. I had always lived surrounded by adults and children a lot older than me. I learned everything I needed to know from them. As far as I was concerned, real life existed around them. Not in the middle of a schoolyard full of terrified children who knew nothing about nothing. From that day on, I detested school. Forever. I'm not setting myself up as an example; I simply believe I wasn't made for this. [13]

The other children at school thought Dion was strange and unfriendly. They made fun of her and called her names, including "Vampire," because Dion's eyeteeth were so long that they stuck out of her mouth.

As a child, Dion greatly disliked school and felt she did not belong there.

Her Real Life

Dion wasn't interested in academics either. "I could never answer anything at school anyway. Even when I pass a school today, I hate it for the kids who are there. School was taking me away from my family and friends and destiny. Every day I would run home from school as fast as I could. I couldn't wait to come back to the basement and hear [the others] rehearse every day." [14] In 1991, Dion told a Canadian interviewer, "At school I was sleeping and dreaming all the time. I didn't learn anything. For me, singing was the *real* life, not two plus two equals four." [15]

Staying up late at Le Vieux Baril also made it hard for Dion to concentrate in school. "I often went to bed very late. I ate when I was hungry. I slept when there were no more people playing music. I missed school regularly, or if I did go, I was so tired that I nodded out during class. . . . I could hardly open my eyes and follow what was going on in class, so I dreamed . . . that I'd be on a big stage one day, the doors to recording studios would fly open for me, and I'd be a big singing star." [16] To keep her from falling behind, Dion's siblings often did her assignments, while her parents made excuses to authorities for her tardiness and absences. It was not hard for Dion to convince her mother to skip school.

> My mother never said it, but I'm convinced she believed I could learn everything as well at home as I could at school. She had been born in a town in the remotest part of the Gaspé Peninsula [in Quebec], and had learned to read, write, and count with her mother and her elder sisters as her teachers. She wouldn't really say it out loud, but I'm sure she believed that when it comes to education your best teachers are yourself and those you're close to. [17]

School officials became concerned about the shy, quiet girl who could not concentrate on her schoolwork, fell asleep in class, and rarely did her homework. They were afraid that Dion was being neglected or abused by her family, so they asked the local social services department to investigate. "They actually thought I was an abused child!" Dion recalled years later. "Can you believe it? So they sent social workers to our house, where they smelled my mother's cooking, saw all the musical instruments, and heard us all singing, then they knew how much happiness there was."[18] Things might be noisy and chaotic in the Dions' house, but it was clear that young Celine was a cherished member of a devoted family.

The Tale of the Tape

All her life, Dion had dreamed about being a professional singer. Her family realized that she had the talent to do just that. Dion's mother was especially determined to help her daughter achieve her dream.

Thérèse knew that if Dion was to succeed, she needed to do more than perform other people's hits at the family's restaurant. Dion recalled her saying, "You want to be a singer? I want you to do it professionally, with your own songs."[19] She decided that Dion needed a manager who could present her talents to the world.

Dion's efforts to find a manager became a family affair. One day, when Dion was twelve years old, her mother wrote some song lyrics and a simple melody for her. Dion's brother Jacques added a musical arrangement, and the song "Ce n'était qu'un rêve," or "It Was Only a Dream," was finished.

Dion had always performed songs that had already been made popular by other entertainers, and she was thrilled at having an original song to sing. "I was really excited, because, for the first time in my life, I was completely free. Not only could I choose which key to sing this song in, but I could decide which notes to emphasize, which syllables to lengthen or trill. It would be my first real song."[20]

Dion recorded a demo tape of "It Was Only a Dream" and another song her mother wrote, "Grand-maman" ("Grandmother"), on a cheap tape recorder in the family kitchen. Her family decided to send the tape to René Angelil, the most important record producer in Quebec. His most important client was Ginette Reno, a French-Canadian singer who had recorded the biggest-selling record in Canada in the late 1970s. Reno was also Dion's idol, and she and her family felt that Dion's talents would be a good fit with Angelil.

Thérèse wrapped the demo tape in brown paper with a red bow, and a friend of Dion's brother who worked in the music industry delivered the tape to Angelil's office. Then the family waited for Angelil to call. But he did not. Dion recalls those tense days:

After about two weeks, there was still no news. Out of fear of missing René Angelil's call, my mother made sure that someone was in the house at all times. . . . I was really disappointed that we hadn't heard anything, but she was furious.[21]

Dion's brother Michel was just as annoyed and impatient. "All he'd have to do is hear you one time, and he wouldn't think twice about taking you on,"[22] he said. Michel had met Angelil several times, so he called Angelil's office repeatedly until he finally got him on the phone. "I know you haven't listened to the demo my sister sent you," he told Angelil, "'cause if you had, you would have already called us. . . . My sister is twelve, but she's no little girl. She's a real singer. Listen to her and you'll see. What'll it take, ten minutes? And it could change your life."[23]

Michel hung up. Ten minutes later, the phone rang. It was Réne Angelil. He had listened to the tape and wanted Dion to come to his office as soon as possible.

Ginette Reno

Ginette Reno was one of René Angelil's first clients and one of Quebec's most popular musical stars. She was also Dion's idol and inspiration when she was a young singer growing up.

Reno was born Ginette Raynault in Montreal on April 28, 1946. She began her singing career at the age of fourteen, performing at amateur contests and other local events. When she was still a teenager, Reno appeared in many Montreal nightclubs and on Quebec television and radio programs as well. Because she sang in both French and English, her popularity spread to parts of Canada outside Quebec. In 1972 and 1973, she won two Juno Awards for Outstanding Female Performance of the Year.

Reno's popularity spread throughout Europe after she hosted a series of television programs in England in 1969. She toured the United States in the early 1970s, and also appeared on a number of popular U.S. talk shows hosted by Johnny Carson, Merv Griffin, and Dinah Shore.

In 1977, Reno formed her own record company, and in 1980, she left Angelil's management to handle her own affairs. Reno has been called "the soul of music" and one of the greatest entertainers in the world, but many people in the industry have said she is difficult to work with.

A Dream Comes True

Later that same afternoon, Dion and her mother sat in Angelil's office in Montreal. Angelil told Dion that he had listened to the tape and thought her voice was beautiful. Then he asked Dion to sing for him. He handed Dion a pen and told her to pretend it was a microphone.

Dion recalled the moment in her autobiography:

> I'd done this hundreds of times in front of my bedroom mirror. But then I could see myself singing, and I had tapes for accompaniment. I'd also sung dozens of times in amateur contests and playgrounds. But I'd never sung into empty space, in front of two people, without music, in front of a sad-looking guy whom I hardly knew. I knew I just had to dive into it, start singing. There was no other choice. . . . I

Who Is René Angelil?

Although few people in the United States had heard of René Angelil before Celine Dion became a superstar, he was well known in the Quebec music industry for many years. Angelil is famous as a manager, but his first success came as a performer.

René Angelil was born in Quebec on January 16, 1942. His father was Syrian and his mother was French Canadian. Angelil's father had always worked at low-paying jobs, and the family encouraged Angelil to have a brighter future by becoming a lawyer or an accountant.

During the early 1960s, Angelil worked in a bank and became interested in international finance. He taught himself to speak several languages, including English. However, Angelil was also passionate about music. Along with two classmates, he formed a rock group called Les Baronets ("The Barons"). As the band became more popular, Angelil left school to pursue music full-time.

At that time, the Beatles were extremely popular all over the world. Les Baronets played the same type of music as the Beatles and appealed to the same teenage audience. The only difference was that Les Baronets performed in French! Soon the group was hugely popular in Quebec and had many hit singles there.

Despite the group's success, Angelil soon tired of the rock star lifestyle. He was especially bothered by the widespread abuse of drugs and alcohol. In 1973, Angelil quit Les Baronets and became a promoter, manager, and producer of many popular Quebec musicians.

René Angelil was impressed with what he heard on Dion's demo tape and immediately wanted to be her manager.

brought the pen to my lips and began singing. All of a sudden I was feeling very good and confident.[24]

Angelil recalled their meeting:

You wouldn't say she was a cute child, but she had these incredible brown eyes. I asked her to pretend she was in front of 2,000 people. When I handed her the pen to use as a microphone, she closed her eyes and she was there. I had goose bumps listening to her voice, so full of feeling, and older than her years. In the end I was crying.[25]

When Dion saw that Angelil had tears in his eyes, "I then told myself that we had him. I'd never seen a man cry while listening to someone sing."[26]

As soon as Dion finished singing, Angelil told her and Thérèse that he wanted to be her manager. They signed a contract, and Angelil told Thérèse he would make her daughter a star within five years. Celine Dion's life was about to change forever.

Chapter 2

Taking the Challenge

Having René Angelil's support and guidance was a tremendous boost to Dion's career. However, his efforts were just one part of what would make her successful. Once again, family support would play an important role in her future. And Dion herself had plenty to do as well. She knew that everyone would have to work together if she was to become a star. "You can have the biggest talent in the world," she said, "but if you don't have the team and the timing—because I believe in destiny—to be there at the right time with the right song, it just won't happen." [27]

Believing in Celine

René Angelil immediately jumped into action. He decided that Dion should re-record "It Was Only a Dream" and "Grand-maman" in a professional recording studio. At that first recording session, Dion got her first taste of Angelil's high expectations when he told the technicians, "Wait and hear her sing. It'll knock you out." [28]

Dion was embarrassed. After all, she was just a child at her first recording session, and these technicians had worked with many professional singers who had much more experience than she had. In her autobiography, she explained:

> I'd soon learn that René always had very high expectations, or should I say, expectations that are too high. It's pretty terrifying—even if it's motivating—creating for you the biggest challenges you can imagine. . . . All this buildup definitely gave me the feeling that if I flopped that evening, if I "bombed" with such experienced people, maybe everything between us would come to an end. In that case, I

would have only given half, a quarter of myself. But luckily I'm the type of singer who forgets everything after the first few notes and discovers an enormous confidence in herself. [29]

Dion's session went well, and the recording was enough to convince several top musicians and songwriters to work with her. Angelil also hired Cecile Jalbert, a famous vocal coach in Quebec, to polish Dion's style and smooth the rough edges in her voice. Dion's voice was rich and powerful, but she had much to learn. In addition to developing a sense of when to emphasize a word or phrase and when to hold back, she needed help with technical details. Jalbert began to teach her breath control, as well as how to support her voice by singing from her diaphragm rather than her throat, and special techniques that would be necessary when Dion went into the recording studio.

Angelil thought Dion could be very successful and hired a voice coach for her.

Angelil also decided that Dion would record two albums at the same time, not just one. One album would contain emotional ballads, and the other would be a collection of Christmas songs. Angelil oversaw every production detail, from hiring the backup singers and instrumentalists to supervising the audio engineers and mixers He even told songwriter Eddy Marnay what type of songs to write for Dion. Marnay was a well-known French songwriter who had written for some of France's most popular entertainers. He got along well with Dion and said she had "the voice of God." [30]

Angelil believed so strongly in Dion's talent that he put his own future on the line for her. Dion's family did not know it when they asked him to represent Celine, but Angelil's biggest star, Ginette Reno, had recently left his management firm to go out on her own. Angelil was devastated by the loss, and even considered leaving the music business, until he heard Dion sing. Dion's voice inspired Angelil so much that within six months, he stopped working with his other clients so he could focus completely on her.

Losing Reno also meant that Angelil did not have enough money to pay for recording and promoting Dion's music. To finance Dion's career, Angelil convinced his wife to mortgage their house. If Dion's records did not sell, the Angelils could lose their home. Writer Martin Melhuish explained just how risky this was, and how it showed Angelil's commitment to Dion:

> I always have a great deal of respect for managers who take an act and put their lives on the line with that act. It either works or it fails. It works or you both fail. This [mortgaging the house] was total belief on his part. . . . When you mortgage your house for something that's in the entertainment business, you're taking the ultimate chance. Because of the failure rate. [31]

High Expectations

On June 19, 1981, Dion made her first television appearance on a popular Quebec talk show hosted by Michel Jasmin. Thirteen-year-old Dion astonished Jasmin and the audience with her powerful

Angelil and Dion pose in front of the Canadian Walk of Fame. The two have worked together since Dion was twelve years old.

Becoming a Star in the Record Industry

Just because musicians write or perform fantastic songs does not mean they can have a hit record. The music industry is a big, complicated business. A lot of money is at stake, and often music itself is treated as a product rather than a creative work.

To become successful, musicians need to find people to manage their careers. Managers make it their business to meet important people in the industry, such as record producers, executives, and radio programmers. In this way, they develop the connections that are necessary to find a record company that is willing to distribute their clients' work. Managers and promoters meet regularly with record company executives to discuss their clients, and also showcase their musicians at industry trade shows and conventions.

Even a record deal with a widely distributed label does not guarantee that a hopeful musician will become a star. Record companies work heavily to promote their records, but most of the money is put behind artists who are already stars, whose new releases are almost guaranteed to be successful. Newer or less popular acts receive less promotional money and, therefore, less attention.

voice. Before the show, Dion waited nervously backstage with Angelil. She was shaking with fear, until Angelil whispered, "Go ahead, show them you're the best."[32] Dion's stage fright disappeared as soon as she started to sing, and her performance was a huge success.

Dion was comfortable onstage, but she was not sure what to say during her on-camera interview with Jasmin. When he asked her if she planned to take singing lessons, she answered

> rather abruptly, as if it were obvious that I didn't need any lessons. I don't know why I answered like that. . . . My answer must have seemed ridiculously pretentious. . . . But I so wanted to become a great singer that I'd begun to think I had everything I needed to do so. I believed so strongly in myself that modesty seemed to disappear as soon as the subject was my voice. . . . René encouraged that attitude in me, and I don't think he was shocked or bothered by what I'd said to Michel Jasmin. . . . "If you want to go far, you have to know what you can do and

you have to tell it to the world. That way, you've got no other choice but to do it." That's what he thought.[33]

Quebec Superstar

The summer of 1981 was a busy one for Dion. She recorded two albums and also sang the national anthems of the United States and Canada before baseball games at the Olympic Stadium in Montreal.

In November 1981, *La voix du bon dieu (Good God's Voice)* and *Celine chante Nöel (Celine Sings Christmas)* were released on Angelil's own record label. The albums were an instant success and sold more than thirty thousand copies by the end of the year.

For Dion, the hard work of the past year was just the beginning. She and Angelil began a relentless schedule of photo shoots, autographing sessions, personal appearances, and radio and television appearances to keep her name and image in the public eye. She quickly became a rising star in the Quebec music scene. And she

Airplay: The Key to a Hit

Radio airplay is a key ingredient in having a hit record. Just as managers try to convince record companies to take an interest in their clients, record companies work hard to get the attention of radio programmers. Stations in large cities, such as New York and Los Angeles, are especially influential because they reach an audience of millions of people. Record companies send tapes and information about their artists to programmers at these large stations, hoping that the programmers will add the songs to their playlist. Once artists receive airplay at these large stations, their music will also be played at other stations around the country.

Programmers base their airplay decisions on what they think will be popular, but sometimes they make mistakes. In 2001, stations refused to play Sting's song, "Desert Rose," because programmers felt the song's opening—a chant by Algerian singer Cheb Mami—would not appeal to American audiences. However, when the song was featured in a commercial for Jaguar cars, listeners flooded radio stations with requests for the song. Programmers hurried to add "Desert Rose" to their playlists, and the song went on to become a hit record in the United States.

did not mind the hard work, because she knew it was the only way to achieve her goals. She remembered the words her mother often told her: "You get nothing for nothing."[34]

In 1982, Dion, her mother, and Angelil traveled to France to record her third album, *Tellement j'ai d'amour pour toi (I Have So Much Love for You)*. Dion sang the title song directly to Thérèse during the recording session to let her know how much her mother's love and support meant to her. "I know my mother well, and she doesn't cry easily. . . . But it was clear she was very moved, proud of me, glad, happy about the path we'd taken,"[35] Dion said of that moment.

Dion's third album sold more than fifty thousand copies in Canada. It was also a hit in France, and Dion became the first Canadian artist to have a gold record in France.

The World of Quebec

Most music critics agree that growing up in Quebec provided a tremendous boost to Dion's career. The Quebec music scene is very

A couple in Montreal dances to a street musician. Quebec is a province known for supporting its local musicians.

active and good at promoting local acts. One Canadian writer, Norman Provencher, said that "Quebec's star-making machine has always been better oiled and more efficient than the entertainment scene in the rest of Canada. The close-knit organization of rabid tabloids and small regional clubs and entertainment halls can, and do, create big (and quite wealthy) fish in the small pond in no time." [36] Another music journalist, Martin Melhuish, points out that

> Quebeckers are one of the highest per capita purchasers of records in the world. It is not uncommon to find a big hit in Quebec selling more records than in the rest of Canada combined. Much of the credit for this enthusiasm has to go to the star system that exists in Quebec because of the heavy exposure generated by newspapers, fan magazines, TV, and radio. This is another part of the scene that Dion came out of. They had a built-in star system there. . . . The newspapers got behind her and TV and everything else. The big difference between Quebec and the rest of Canada is the media. [37]

Quebec also had a reputation for promoting child stars. Young performers such as Ginette Reno and René Simard became huge stars in Quebec and used their success to launch popular careers in Europe. Although artists such as Reno and Simard were not very well known in the United States—or even in English-speaking parts of Canada—they were extremely popular in Quebec.

Dion was also helped by a government ruling that stated 30 percent of the songs played on the radio and 80 percent of television shows be performed or written by Canadians. Known as "Con Can," for "Canadian content" (*contenu canadien* in French), this law helps preserve Canada's culture and keeps its artists from being overshadowed by artists from the United States or Europe.

Nicknames

After Dion received a gold record in France, her popularity at home increased. Quebec radio stations began playing her songs more frequently. "She did what every Quebec singer dreams of," [38] Jean-Claude Aubin, a Canadian record executive, said of

Dion's success. The media gave Dion an affectionate nickname, "la petite quebecoise," which means "the little girl from Quebec."

Dion's prominent eyeteeth, which had caused her so much teasing in school, gave her a less friendly nickname: "Canine Dion." Even though she was a recording star, she was still just a teenager, and jokes about her appearance hurt Dion. "I used to cover my mouth with my hand on stage. No seriously, it was a big problem then, with my public, with photographers. I would listen to some comedian making fun of my teeth on television and I used to cry."[39]

Soon Dion stopped smiling for photographs in an effort to hide her teeth. Her mother sympathized with her. "Many 15-year-old girls have to fix their teeth," Thérèse said. "But for Celine it was a real problem, all these people laughing at her. You know how young girls are."[40] It would be several years and many triumphs later before Dion could find the time to have extensive dental work done on those "vampire teeth."

Music Is Everything

Dion's growing success was a dream come true for the teenager. Her life became a whirlwind of recording sessions, concert tours, and personal appearances. Finally, she was able to devote her life completely to music and the entertainment business.

For Dion, one of the best parts of being a professional singer was that it provided an escape from school. As soon as she turned professional, Angelil hired a tutor to teach Dion outside of the classroom. Following the laws regarding how many hours a day child performers must attend school, this teacher worked privately with Dion whenever she was not recording or performing.

Dion preferred working one-on-one with an adult rather than being in a classroom with children her own age. But she still was bored by schoolwork and did not put much effort into her studies. "School was taking me away from my happiness, from my dreams,"[41] she later explained. On the rare occasions when Dion was home, she would return to school but "every time I went there, I noticed without much emotion how far I'd fallen behind. I quickly saw that I could never catch up with the others."[42]

When she was sixteen, Dion could legally leave school, and she did. "I was not very comfortable at school. I hated it. I couldn't learn. I was dreaming, I couldn't concentrate, because I was learning stuff I knew I was not going to use. School is not for everybody, I believe, and I didn't like it. I'm going to the school of life and I'm learning much more."[43]

In her autobiography, Dion would later emphasize that her lack of schooling was not something other young people should follow. "The world has changed a lot since I was a teenager," she wrote. "Except for very rare exceptions, I don't believe you can get by and feel good about yourself without an education."[44]

A New Kind of Education

Even though she was no longer in school, Dion was still learning. René Angelil wanted her to learn everything she could about the

Dion dropped out of school at the age of sixteen to pursue her music career.

entertainment world. "He was determined to teach me show business: the methodology of show business, the history of show business, the geography and economics of show business. . . . I became the most studious little girl in the world."[45]

Dion also followed a rigorous program of vocal exercises. She continued to take voice lessons and spent at least thirty-five minutes a day on exercises to strengthen and maintain her voice. Dion often spent two hours leaning over a pot of boiling water and breathing in the steam. This steam treatment keeps vocal cords from becoming dry and helps the voice recover from overuse. Whenever possible she went to bed early to rest her voice.

In addition to learning about the business and taking voice lessons, Angelil had her watch videos of her performances over and over again, so she could see how she looked. Although Dion had sung at Le Vieux Baril for years, she did not have the polish of a seasoned performer, and she sometimes looked awkward. Angelil and Dion observed and discussed how Dion moved, held the microphone, and interacted with the audience.

> What he really wanted was for me to get used to seeing myself and to become comfortable with looking at myself—as if I were a part of the audience. It isn't easy to do this. But you really have to. For years, René put me through this exercise every time I went on TV. I had to envision the broadcast and watch myself singing, which was more terrifying for me than facing big audiences. If certain things seemed like a disaster to me, I quickly corrected them and didn't think about them anymore. . . . I watched myself five, six times.[46]

Vocal Discipline

Dion also developed very disciplined work habits so that her voice would always be in good shape. She never smoked or took drugs, and did not drink alcohol. She did not even drink cold tea or soda, or eat spicy foods, because these, too, might harm her voice. As a rule she usually went to bed early rather than attend parties. Taking care of her voice has always been Dion's top priority.

Dion takes care of her voice by performing vocal exercises and avoiding smoke, alcohol, and spicy foods.

Every day, I take care of my voice. There's no air conditioning, even if it's summer and I'm sweating. If people are smoking, I have to ask them to stop. I can't go out because if you go to a discotheque, everybody's screaming and you have to talk louder, and you have no voice for the next morning. So this is discipline. But, with time, you do it naturally. For me, the only thing on my mind is my voice and my career. This is my life. . . . There's one way to do showbiz—if you want to do it perfectly, you have to be disciplined and you have to be ready to work really hard.[47]

Angelil compared Dion's work ethic with that of an Olympic athlete. Dion recalled that he told reporters "how I practiced my songs in my head, and said that a singer, like an athlete, has to train every day so that her vocal cords stay in shape."[48]

Dion's dedication to her career meant she could not have a normal teenage life, but she had no regrets about what she missed. "Kids today want to go out and go to clubs and have a drink and

Vocal Exercises

Just as athletes must stretch and keep their bodies in shape if they want to perform to the best of their abilities, singers must exercise their voices. Before a rehearsal or a concert, singers "warm up" by singing scales and other vocal exercises that slowly extend the voice to the upper and lower ranges. These exercises are especially important for professional singers who may perform for several hours day after day. Without these exercises, vocal cords can become damaged or strained. This can lead to hoarseness or laryngitis. In addition, small growths called polyps may develop on damaged vocal cords. Usually these growths must be removed surgically, followed by a long period of recuperation. After surgery, some singers' voices are never the same.

try to smoke and have boyfriends," she told *Time* magazine in 1994. "Since I wanted to be onstage, I had to go to bed early. You can't have everything. You have to make a choice."[49]

A Major Challenge in Tokyo

In October 1982, Dion received some wonderful news. Her song, "Tellement j'ai d'amour pour toi" was chosen to represent France in the Yamaha World Song Festival in Tokyo, Japan. More than two thousand songs from all over the world had been submitted to this very important event.

As usual, Angelil made it clear that he knew Dion would do her best. "I know you're the best singer who'll be over there," he told her on the night they found out Dion's song would be in the competition. "And you know you'll win first prize—don't you?"[50]

Dion traveled to Tokyo with her mother, Angelil, and several others. Dion performed her song in front of twelve thousand people at an auditorium called the Budokan and made it to the finals, which were held the following afternoon.

As she prepared for the finals, Dion was overcome by stage fright. Not only would she be performing in front of twelve thousand people again, but the contest would be televised to millions of people. "Waves of anguish washed over me as I thought of the moment when I'd have to go onstage and launch into my song. I imagined the crowd I'd have to face as a heartless monster capable of devouring me. And I tried to forget, to tell myself that this wasn't so important, that I'd survive very well without taking home first prize."[51] Angelil knew Dion would overcome her fears.

> René didn't try at all to convince me that I had no reason to be afraid. On the contrary, he kept telling me that this was a crucial, decisive moment in my life, that the monster I was about to face was terrible. He knew it was. But he added that I had no choice, that I had to win. Instead of diminishing this monster, as I'd been trying to do, he told me that I was strong, determined, capable of facing it. When he spoke to me, I really felt like a great person, a real professional. That evening I went to bed convinced that once I got onstage I'd know how to master my voice. And tame the monster. Maybe even knock it out.[52]

Dion did "knock out" the monster. When the awards were announced, Dion won Best Artist and the Gold Medal for Best Song. Dion was so happy, "I cried a lot. On the stage, in front of

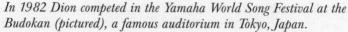

In 1982 Dion competed in the Yamaha World Song Festival at the Budokan (pictured), a famous auditorium in Tokyo, Japan.

the audience at the Budokan and the Japanese television viewers. Then in the wings, I found René too crying as though his heart would break. And Maman [mother, was crying also] . . . . Our interpreter and the Japanese people around us looked like they were in shock. I don't think they were used to seeing such public displays of emotion."[53]

Superstar

When Dion returned to Quebec after her triumph in Tokyo, she was greeted as a superstar. A crowd met her at the airport, and reporters visited her at home. She met the prime minister of Quebec and was invited to sing at a huge show in the Montreal Forum, along with many other popular artists. At the age of fourteen, Dion had become one of the most popular stars in Quebec's history.

Early in 1983, Dion, her mother, and Angelil traveled to France, where Dion would sing at Midem, an international meeting of the record industry. Midem was the biggest recording fair in the world, and all the best producers, composers, and journalists would be there. Dion's records had not been selling as well in France as they had in Quebec, and Angelil knew that a successful appearance at Midem could make Dion a huge star in France.

As usual, Angelil made sure Dion knew how important this performance would be. "I understood that, this time, if my song didn't make it in France . . . I'd be out of the game altogether. And surprisingly enough, I was excited by such high stakes, by this last and only chance I had no choice but to seize."[54]

Dion put on a powerful, astonishing performance that received a standing ovation from the music industry representatives. Dion's song was added to radio station playlists, and she was invited to appear on a popular French television show hosted by Michel Drucker. Drucker was so influential that a press agent told Dion, "If he speaks to you even for only thirty seconds, you'll know that you've become a big star in Europe."[55]

Drucker watched Dion sing her new single, "D'amour ou d'amitie" ("Love or Friendship") in rehearsal and congratulated her. Dion was thrilled, but Angelil had a different reaction. "René really didn't want me to declare victory too soon," she wrote in her auto-

Michel Drucker, pictured with French TV entertainer Julie Snyder, contributed to Dion's success by having her appear on his show when she was fifteen years old.

biography. "I could see he wasn't too pleased that Michel Drucker had come to congratulate me so quickly. He wanted to up the ante. 'That doesn't mean that you've made the grade,' he said. 'You have to impress him even more. . . .' More and more, that's what René was asking for. I was still very young, but I knew that the higher the ante, the higher I'd go."[56]

Dion did respond to the pressure, and her appearance on Drucker's show was a huge success. By the time the fifteen-year-old left Paris later that week, her song was at the top of the music charts, and she was Europe's new singing sensation.

By 1986, Dion was on top of the French-speaking world. She had released nine albums, which sold $10 million in Quebec and France. She also won fifteen Felix Awards, which are the French-Canadian equivalent of the Grammies. The Felix Awards are given by the Association of Recording and Performing Industries in Quebec, which is known by the French acronym Adisq. During her first appearance at the Adisq ceremonies, she won four Felix Awards and amused critics by crying hysterically each time she went up to accept. "The next day, the main paper of Quebec showed my face swollen with tears and all puffy from sobbing," Dion recalled a few years later. "A lot of girls are moved to tears when they walk up to receive a prize, but I think I hold the absolute crying record. For two or three years, my crying jags were the delight of critics and commentators in Quebec."[57]

One of the high points of Dion's early career was singing for Pope John Paul II during his visit to Montreal in 1984. She performed her song "La colombe" ("The Dove") in front of the pope

Dion performed for Pope John Paul II when he visited Montreal in 1984.

and sixty-five thousand people at a youth rally in Olympic Stadium. The following October, Dion and Angelil had a private audience with the pope in Rome. "It was an experience we'll never forget," Angelil told reporters. "Though it only lasted a few minutes, we're still having trouble believing it happened at all." [58]

Singing for the pope and later meeting him personally were thrilling experiences for Dion, who was raised as a Roman Catholic. Despite her position as a musical star, in many ways, Dion was still a simple, small town girl at heart.

By 1986, Dion was eighteen years old. She had been a child star for her entire career, but now she was no longer a child. She and Angelil agreed that it was time for a major change.

Chapter 3

Conquering America

BY 1986, DION was the hottest star in Quebec, and she was also popular in France. However, all her recordings were in French. Because of the language barrier, few English-speaking people in Canada knew who she was. And in the United States, which is the largest entertainment market in the world, she was a complete unknown.

To appeal to a wider, more sophisticated audience, Dion and Angelil knew that in addition to overcoming the language barrier, Dion would have to change the style of music she sang. "At the beginning of my career, I was always regarded as a little child," Dion said. "I sang mostly ballads, which I still love, but my audience was mostly children and very old people. It was always very difficult for me to get my records played on the major pop stations. Which is part of the reason I decided to change my look and my style."[59]

Another challenge was that Dion had been a child star, but now she was growing up. Most child stars, whether in movies, television, or music, find it hard to continue their success when they grow up. If Dion was to continue to be a star, she had to transform herself and her music to appeal to a whole new audience.

Many Changes

Angelil came up with a comprehensive plan to change Dion's image and style. First, she would take eighteen months off from performing and recording. "If Celine was going to become a great artist and not just another minor one who grew up, she had to stop completely in order to allow the image that she had to fade. There was risk in changing her image, but it wasn't all that great because I knew how talented she was,"[60] Angelil explained.

Although Dion would be out of the public eye, she would hardly have any time to relax during her sabbatical. First, Dion would learn to speak and sing in English. She enrolled in a two-month language course. For eight hours a day, five days a week, Dion studied her new language. During class, she only spoke English. Angelil had thought it would take a year for Dion to learn English, but her dedication and hard work in this intensive course allowed her to become proficient in just a few months. Her ear for music probably helped as well, since Celine was adept at recognizing and mimicking speech rhythms and accents.

However, some of the details of English proved hard for the young woman to master. "The biggest problem I had was when you go to school to learn English, they teach you the perfect way: 'How do you do?' and 'How are you?' Then you go out on the street, and you think you speak English, and you hear, 'Hey, mama, yo, mama, yo, whassup?' It's like, 'Oh, my God, it's not in the dictionary.' I was looking for 'Yo, mama, yo,' and it was not there."[61]

For a long time, Dion felt insecure speaking a new language. "When people make jokes in English, I laugh because I want to be nice," she admitted. "But sometimes I don't understand everything, or else I really want to say something but it doesn't come out as well as I want."[62] With time and practice, however, Dion eventually became fluent in English.

During her eighteen-month break from performing, Dion continued to listen to a variety of popular music. She needed to broaden her musical horizons to include not only ballads, but up-tempo rock songs as well.

Dion also went through a personal transformation. She wore braces and had her protruding teeth capped, cut and styled her hair, began wearing makeup, and changed her wardrobe. Instead of long dresses that made her look like a sweet little girl, Dion started appearing in tighter, more revealing clothes.

A New Celine

In 1987, Dion returned to recording and performing. During her sabbatical, Angelil had been busy arranging a new record deal for her. He convinced an executive at CBS Music (now Sony Music) to distribute her next album. CBS was one of the largest record companies in the world, and the home of superstars such as Michael Jackson, Barbra Streisand, Julio Iglesias, and Bruce Springsteen.

Angelil also arranged for younger songwriters to write the music for Dion's next album. These songwriters had a more modern style that would appeal to a wider audience.

In 1987, Dion released *Incognito* on the CBS label. A press release for the album announced the new Dion image by saying, "When youth, beauty, and talent come together in one package, the results are explosive."[63] Although the album was in French, it showed Dion's new style and attitude. The album was very different from her previous work, and it showed that she could sing upbeat rock and dance tunes as well as ballads. *Incognito* raced up the Canadian and European charts and produced many hit singles.

Barbra Streisand, shown here holding her Golden Globe Award, recorded albums with CBS Music, the same company Dion signed a recording contract with in 1987.

Eurovision Song Contest

Although it is little known in the United States, the Eurovision song contest is one of the most important musical competitions in the world. The competition is set up like an Olympic event. Countries are represented by songwriters, who can choose anyone they like to perform their song. (This is why the Canadian Dion represented Switzerland in the 1988 Eurovision contest.) Judges award points after each singer performs, and the top scorers move on to the finals. The winners receive instant recognition throughout Europe and often go on to have successful careers there.

Some of the artists who have been featured at Eurovision include ABBA, Julio Iglesias, and Olivia Newton-John. Also, the worldwide phenomenon *Riverdance* was first seen at Eurovision. This dance ensemble was not part of the competition, but was included strictly as entertainment between songs for the audience.

Dion followed the success of *Incognito* with a series of forty-two sold-out shows in Montreal. One Quebec writer noted, "It became clear that Dion had merely picked up where she'd left off—on top."[64]

A Musical Olympics

In 1988, Dion received a phone call from two Swiss songwriters. They had written a song called "Ne partez pas sans moi," or "Don't Leave Without Me," and wanted Dion to sing it in the Eurovision song contest, which would be held in Dublin, Ireland. This contest has been called "Europe's Olympics of song contests" and is broadcast to a television audience of 600 million people around the world. Eurovision has launched the careers of many popular artists, and Dion jumped at the chance to reach such a huge audience.

Dion's performance at the Eurovision contest was phenomenal. The judges gave her top marks, and she won the contest by one point. Winning was an overwhelming experience. Dion "started to cry with joy. After I came back onstage and sang again, I was really frightened because a mob of more than five hundred reporters and photographers threw themselves at me."[65]

The next day, Dion's face was on the front page of most British newspapers, and "Don't Leave Without Me" was being played on radio stations all over Europe. The record went on to sell three hundred thousand copies in Europe and helped popularize Dion in Great Britain and other parts of Europe. Now there was just one more market to conquer.

A New Challenge

Winning the Eurovision contest had been a terrific boost for Dion's career in Europe, but she was still almost completely unknown in the United States. Angelil knew that the only way people there would pay attention to Dion was for her to record an album in English.

Dion and Angelil traveled to Los Angeles, where Dion began working with David Foster, one of the top producers in the music business. For her to record *Unison,* CBS paid $1 million—a huge amount of money in the late 1980s. It was clear that CBS thought Dion could become a major star. CBS president Paul Burger said, "We regard Celine as an incredible opportunity, and we obviously think enough of her to spend whatever it takes to make her a star around the world."[66]

Producer David Foster was impressed by Dion's energy and drive. "Celine's work ethic is near perfect, probably the best I've ever seen,"[67] he said. And Sony record executive Tommy Mottola said of Dion, "I'm amazed at how Celine can continue the kind of schedule she does. She's sort of like the Energizer."[68]

Polly Anthony, president of the Epic Records Group (a division of CBS Records) thinks that Dion's incredible work ethic is a result of her long career. "When you've worked every single day of your life since you were thirteen, there's a tremendous amount of discipline that goes into it."[69]

Journalist Larry LeBlanc agrees, noting, "She's been in training for this since she was a small child. Don't forget . . . by the time she arrived to do her first English album here, which is eight years after she started, she was twenty-one, twenty-two, when she recorded that album. That's eight, nine years of appearing on all those Quebec TV shows, interviews. She was a very poised performer."[70]

Dion herself has a different explanation. She credits her family and their support for her success. "Every time I'm performing, every time I'm doing an interview, every time I'm traveling the world, they're with me and they're in me and I think of them and I do it with so much passion because I love them very much. So I do it for me because I love doing it, but because I love them very much, and I do it for them too."[71]

An extensive publicity campaign was launched, and journalists and radio personalities were flown in to interview Dion. The singer also traveled around the United States to promote the album and its first single, "Where Does My Heart Beat Now?" She appeared on *The Tonight Show,* one of the most popular television shows in the United States. Dion sailed through her U.S. television debut with flying colors and charmed guest host Jay Leno and the audience with her talent.

Tommy Mottola was one of several record producers who thought Dion would be a successful singer in the United States.

Unison—and Division

When *Unison* was released in 1990, it surpassed all expectations. The album became a huge hit in the United States, Canada, and around the world. "Where Does My Heart Beat Now?" reached number four on the charts and stayed in the Top 100 for six months. Her popularity also soared in English-speaking areas of Canada, and she won two Juno Awards for Female Vocalist of the Year and Album of the Year.

Although Dion was thrilled at the success of *Unison,* she also worried that her loyal French-speaking fans in Quebec might turn against her for recording in English. At this time, Quebec was in the middle of a strong nationalistic movement to retain its own language and culture. There was even talk that the province might separate from the rest of Canada. Larry LeBlanc, a writer for *Billboard* magazine, a leading trade paper of the music industry, recalls,

Dion performs at a 1992 concert. Her first English-language album, Unison, *shot to the top of the charts in 1990.*

A Separate Quebec

Quebec is different from other Canadian provinces. Unlike the rest of Canada, Quebecers speak French as their primary language. They also have a strong French-Canadian culture that features values, music, foods, and customs that are very different from the English-speaking areas of the country.

Because it is so distinct from the rest of Canada, many people in Quebec feel the province should be independent. During the 1960s, a strong separatist movement began in the province. This movement grew in popularity during the 1970s. During this time, separatists sometimes used violent methods, such as bombings, to show their feelings. However, the Canadian government and the other provinces felt strongly that Quebec should remain as part of Canada.

In 1980, Quebecers finally got the chance to vote on whether to form a separate nation. Sixty percent voted to stay in Canada. In 1995, 50 percent voted to remain, while 49 percent voted to separate.

During the 1990s, tensions between Quebec and the rest of Canada eased as Canadian officials began treating Quebec as a special province with its own cultural identity. However, the idea of a separate Quebec is still popular with many residents.

It was controversial at the time because you're looking at Celine going into English Canada, learning English at a time of the nationalistic rise of Quebec and the whole question of sovereignty. What I'm saying is even the fact that she sang in English was controversial. . . . To suggest or come out that you were going to go for the approval of the *anglais* in English, singing in English, that was a pretty brave decision.[72]

Dion was so nervous that performing in English would alienate her French-speaking fans that she had nightmares about it. However, she managed to overcome the problem by continuing to record in French and perform in Quebec. Writer Martin Melhuish notes that people in Quebec "thought that she was going to disappear. She proved that wrong. Because she's gone back all the time and continues to record in French. She never abandoned it. . . . She didn't forget where she came from."[73] Indeed, throughout her career Dion has made a point of insisting that "I'm proud to be *quebecoise*. I'm proud to have grown up with the Quebec people."[74]

Dion speaks at a gala in Montreal. Many people in Quebec felt Dion had abandoned her French-speaking fans because she recorded songs in English.

In a 1992 interview with *Maclean's* magazine, she spoke of that pride, saying, "I'll always be a Quebecker-Canadian. I'm from Quebec and every time I go to a country I say that. It's my roots, my origins and it's the most important thing to me."[75]

Despite her loyalty to Quebec, it did not take long for Dion's new English-speaking career to get her into trouble. In 1990, Dion was nominated for a Felix Award for Anglophone Artist of the Year. This award was specifically given to English-speaking performers. Dion and Angelil were insulted by the nomination, because to them it indicated that the Adisq and the Quebec music industry felt she had "sold out" and abandoned her French-speaking fans. Newspapers in Quebec felt the same way and attacked Dion for competing in an English category.

Dion attended the ceremony and won the Felix for Anglophone Artist. However, she shocked the audience when she went onstage and announced, "I cannot accept this award. I think my fans understand that I am not an Anglophone artist. . . . Everywhere I go, I say I'm proud to be *quebecoise*."[76] Dion's fans and the Quebec press were thrilled by her actions. However, Adisq was very annoyed and stated, "By refusing the trophy, Dion has refused the encouragement of those who have witnessed her career from its beginnings, and who have always supported it."[77]

Although *Unison* was very successful, many critics felt that Dion's work in English was not as powerful as her French recordings. Dion had been singing in French since she was a child, and it was clear that she was more comfortable singing in French than in English. She understood the French lyrics deeply, and therefore she could put more emotion and meaning behind them. Dion's live performances were also more energized and passionate in front of French-speaking audiences. Writer Larry LeBlanc said that "I don't think she was served well on her first two English albums because her English wasn't good enough. She didn't know what . . . she was singing on the first album. If you really notice, on the first two albums, there's not much nuance in the voice. . . . However, you get into her French albums and they touch her soul."[78] However, as Dion became more familiar and comfortable with the English language, her performances improved.

A Personal Challenge

No sooner had the turmoil from the Felix Awards blown over than Dion faced a new crisis. She came down with a case of laryngitis that would not go away. Then, during a concert in Sherbrooke, Canada, Dion lost her voice entirely. "It came apart like wet paper,"[79] she recalled. It seemed that her incredible career might be over just as it was truly taking off.

Dion consulted throat specialists in Montreal and New York City. They told her to rest her voice completely. For the next three weeks, Dion did not say a word. Instead, she communicated by writing notes or tapping out a code on the telephone (one fingernail tap for yes, two taps for no). Dion still

Dion helps protect her voice by drinking fluids during her concerts.

uses these methods today, because she rarely speaks on the day of a concert.

The doctors also gave Dion a program of vocal exercises and told her that she would have to work even harder to avoid irritants such as cigarette smoke, dust, and pollution, as well as stress and fatigue, which can also damage the voice. Dion dedicated herself to caring for her voice. She never missed her vocal exercises, which took thirty-five minutes a day, and became a fanatic about protecting her voice from any irritants. Angelil admired her commitment. "When Celine stopped singing for the sheer joy of it in the car, in the plane, wherever she was, I knew she had what counted to be a star,"[80] he said. Once again, Dion's determination had saved her career.

Celine Dion, Businesswoman

Music was not the only way Dion was making her mark during the 1990s. Shortly after *Unison* was released, Angelil began looking for ways to invest the huge sums of money Dion was making. Because Dion loved to cook and enjoyed old-fashioned styles of food, Angelil decided that a restaurant would be an excellent investment.

Dion and Angelil worked with several experts in the restaurant industry to create a chain of restaurants called Nickels. Nickels copies the styles of the 1950s, serving such favorites as cheeseburgers, chicken sandwiches, French fries, and milkshakes. Menu items are named after 1950s celebrities, such as "the Elvis Special" (a

Selling Her Image

Dion has used more than her powerful voice to make records. She has also lent her name and image to several corporate sponsors. In 1988, Dion signed a three-year contract with Chrysler Canada to promote the company's cars in Quebec. Dion appeared in television commercials, in newspaper and radio ads, and on billboards. In 1991, Dion promoted Diet Coke in exchange for the Coca-Cola Company's sponsorship of her tour. Later, Dion promoted American Express and Procter and Gamble.

Dion is certainly not the first star to use her image to sell products completely unrelated to music. Many stars take on this role because it is a lucrative way to make money. Others rely on major corporations to sponsor tours, which can cost millions of dollars to produce.

double cheeseburger). Dion did name one menu item after herself—a six-layer chocolate cake called "Celine." The restaurants are
also decorated in the style of the 1950s, and feature vinyl booths,
old cars and motorcycles, jukeboxes, and pictures of Presley,
Marilyn Monroe, James Dean, and other 1950s icons. There are
also displays of Dion's own memorabilia, such as records, cos-
tumes, and awards. The dessert menu is shaped like a record.

The first Nickels opened on December 5, 1990, in St. Laurent, a
suburb of Montreal. Since then, the company has become very successful. As of 1997, there were forty-five Nickels locations, mostly in
Quebec, serving more than 6 million people a year.

Dion has taken an active role in Nickels. Along with being part
of the management team, she designed the staff's uniforms (bobby
socks, sneakers, and pink skirts for the waitresses). She also makes
personal appearances at the restaurants. Nickels is also a family affair. Dion's mother and one of her brothers own and operate two of
the restaurants, and Dion's sisters Linda and Claudette, as well as her
niece Brigitte, are on the staff.

Chapter 4

True Love—and Heartache

CELINE DION AND René Angelil had been together almost every day since she was just twelve years old. Angelil was twenty-six years older than Dion, and married, when they first met. Over the years, however, Angelil and his wife would divorce, and his relationship with Dion would become much more than professional.

Celine's Secret

As a young teenager, Dion always felt safe, secure, and protected by Angelil's guidance. After a concert, Angelil usually came to Dion's dressing room or hotel room and told her and her mother how he felt the evening had gone. When he left, he always kissed both women on the cheek. In her autobiography, Dion recalled those friendly kisses. "I'd go to bed with my cheeks softly tingling—and with a little of his cologne on my skin."[81]

Dion told no one—not even her mother—that she was falling in love with Angelil. She was just a teenager and the focus on her career meant she had never had a boyfriend, so she knew no one would take her feelings seriously.

> For the first time in my life, I was hiding something from Maman, hiding my budding love for René. I must have told her at least a hundred times that he was dear to my heart, but I never dared tell her that I dreamed of him every night. . . . I'd found—where I don't know—a photo

Despite their age difference, Dion has loved Angelil since she was a teenager.

of him that I gazed at a thousand times a day without my mother knowing and that I covered with kisses at night, in my bed. I rubbed it against my cheek. It slipped onto my neck like a kiss and slid onto my shoulders. Before I fell asleep, I slipped it under a pillow, out of fear that my mother, who always shared a room with me, would find it.[82]

Dion's situation was complicated by the fact that Angelil clearly was not interested in her personally. "I understood . . . René's head and heart were somewhere else. . . . As soon as I left the stage and work was over, he didn't see me. . . . If he ever spoke to me in a personal way, it was about what I was onstage and TV, about Celine Dion the singer, never about me in real life."[83]

Keeping the secret from her mother was especially hard on Dion. However, her feelings soon became obvious to the people around her, especially those who knew her best—her family. Even the newspapers ran articles and opinion polls about whether Dion and Angelil should be a couple. The gossip and rumors became even more common after Angelil and his wife divorced.

Angelil felt uncomfortable and tried to deny his own feelings toward his young client. One night, as he walked Dion home from dinner, he told her that they could no longer act so friendly to each other. Dion was devastated and tried to get Angelil to say he did not love her. When Angelil did not answer, Dion believed there was still hope.

Dion's mother was upset when she realized how much Dion cared for Angelil. Angelil had been married and divorced twice, and had three children—not the sort of man she had in mind for her youngest child! Dion recalled this painful period of her life in her autobiography:

Not His First Wife

Although Dion's husband René Angelil was her first and only love, Dion is not Angelil's first wife. Angelil had been married twice before. A brief marriage when he was in his twenties produced a son named Patrick. Later, in 1974, Angelil married an actress named Anne, who became the star of a Quebec television show called *Les Tannants (The Troublemakers)*. Anne and René Angelil had a son and daughter, and divorced during the early 1980s, before Angelil began his relationship with Dion.

For the first time in my life, my mother couldn't and didn't want to find a solution to my problem. Worse than that, and despite herself, she'd become an obstacle to my happiness. Far from supporting my love, she wanted to cure me of it, she wanted me to forget René. She even got angry when I talked about him. . . . But at the same time, my mother, a woman of heart, knew that you can't stop a heart from loving. She knew me well enough to understand that I wasn't going to let my feelings for René drop. I had wanted to become a great singer and I was becoming one. I wanted that man in my life; I was going to put as much stubbornness and strength into getting him as I had put into my singing.[84]

Dion finally convinced her mother that her feelings were true, and she truly loved Angelil. One night, when the two were alone in their kitchen at home, Dion suddenly burst into tears and said, "It's true. I love him for real. For life."[85] Her mother responded by hugging her and telling Dion she believed her. Dion "understood then that she was no longer opposed to my project. Maybe she wouldn't go so far as to encourage it, but she had admitted that my passion for René was not just a passing phase. After that day, everything changed."[86]

A Magical Night

Even though she finally had her mother's support, Dion still had to convince Angelil that his feelings for her were real. That moment finally came after Dion won the Eurovision song contest in 1988. After she accepted her award, an emotional Dion ran backstage. "When I found René, I threw myself into his arms and, still crying, hugged him very hard and kissed him on the neck. I was at the height of happiness. He let it happen. He was laughing."[87]

Later, that night, Angelil went to Dion's hotel room to talk to her about the evening, as he always did. Before he left, Dion kissed him on the lips. Angelil hurried from the room, but called on the phone several minutes later and finally admitted that he and Dion belonged together. Dion's dream had finally come true.

The Prison of Lies

Dion and Angelil began living together shortly after the Eurovision contest. Dion should have been happy. But one thing bothered her tremendously. Angelil would not let her tell anyone outside her family that the two were a couple. He was convinced that the media and the public would not approve of their relationship because of the age difference. (At the time, Dion was twenty and Angelil was

At first, Dion and Angelil kept their romantic relationship a secret from the public and the media.

forty-six.) He also feared that people would think he had taken advantage of his position as her manager and was using her. If people reacted negatively to their relationship, Dion's career could be damaged beyond repair.

When the couple returned to Montreal after the Eurovision contest, a reporter asked Dion if she had a boyfriend. She replied that she did not and her career was her top priority. "It was the first of a very long and very painful series of lies," she later wrote. "I was beginning a happy, yet troubled period of my life, the period of my secret love affair. It would bring me great happiness; but despite professional success, the prison of lies I had to lock myself in would from time to time ruin all my pleasure." [88]

Dion was especially troubled by the fact that she sang love songs all the time, yet she could not admit she felt the same passions she sang about.

> On the one hand, in real life, I was supposed to keep claiming that I was a young girl, who knew nothing about love. On the other hand, on stage and screen and in my songs, I was supposed to behave like a mature, fulfilled, much-loved woman. It was just a game, of course, just show business and make-believe. But it was also an upside-down kind of world. Strangely, it was in the world of show business, the world of illusion and fiction, in the songs, videos, photos, where every lie and disguise is allowed, that I was telling the truth. [89]

Dying Too Young

Dion had more to worry about in the early 1990s than her relationship with Angelil. Her sixteen-year-old niece Karine Menard, the daughter of Dion's sister Liette, was terminally ill. Karine had been born with cystic fibrosis and had been sick since she was just a few months old. Dion was especially close to Karine and often took her to concerts and on shopping trips, even though Karine's lungs were so damaged by the disease that she had to carry oxygen tanks with her and was often so weak she had to use a wheelchair.

Karine's illness inspired Dion to raise money for the Cystic Fibrosis Foundation. "I wanted to be part of this foundation when the family learned she [Karine] had cystic fibrosis. I was doing it for her, and I'm still fighting for her,"[90] Dion recalled in an interview with E!Online in 1997.

Dion paid for newspaper ads seeking donations to find a cure for cystic fibrosis. One ad read:

> Dear Friends, when you hear my songs on the radio, when you see me on television, when the newspapers announce to you that I have gained trophies or that I return from Japan, Germany, France . . . you may think, 'That girl is so lucky!' You are right, I consider myself very lucky to live so many beautiful moments. But what would make me happy, more than all the world, would be the discovery, one day, of a remedy for the evil pain my niece Karine suffers from cystic fibrosis. Karine does

Cystic Fibrosis

Cystic fibrosis is one of the most common fatal genetic diseases in the United States. A baby will have cystic fibrosis if each of its parents passes along a defective gene. Approximately thirty thousand American children and young adults have cystic fibrosis. This disease causes the body to secrete a thick, sticky mucus that clogs the lungs and digestive system, making it difficult for victims to breathe or digest food. Eventually, the lungs become so damaged that the patient dies.

Cystic fibrosis is usually diagnosed soon after birth, when the baby has trouble digesting food or gaining weight. Several decades ago, children with this disease usually died before the age of five. However, medical advances and new treatments mean that more than 60 percent of victims live into their thirties or beyond.

Presently, there is no cure for cystic fibrosis. Treatments include physical therapy to dislodge mucus from a patient's lungs, medications that improve breathing, and special diets that help patients absorb more nutrients from their food. Some patients have been helped by lung transplants, although the new lungs will eventually be damaged by the disease, just as the old ones were.

all she can to fight this disease. I want to help her, but I cannot do everything. I need you, your generosity. Research is our only hope. Thank you with all my heart. Celine Dion.[91]

In May 1993, Karine died in Dion's arms. Dion recalled, "I had her in my arms, and I started to sing softly in her ear, and out of nowhere her eyes closed. . . . One tear came down Karine's cheek, and then she was gone."[92]

Karine's death greatly affected Dion. She was hurt, confused, and angry about losing her, and felt it was unfair that the teenager had such a short, painful life and had never known love. Along with raising money to find a cure for cystic fibrosis, Dion has let Karine inspire her in a more personal way. "Karine made me discover and explore an entire world of emotion I would never have known without her. For me she isn't dead, and she never will be. I always feel her very near, helping me, inspiring me, lighting up my life."[93] In a television interview, Dion explained that Karine "put me in contact with heaven, and that is probably the biggest gift that somebody can give you."[94]

The Secret Is Out

Nineteen ninety-three was a sad year for Dion, but it also brought her tremendous personal happiness. After five years of keeping her relationship with René Angelil a secret, Dion was finally able to tell the world that they were in love.

The disclosure of their relationship began with a song. Dion was working on her third English album, *The Color of My Love*. Dion told Angelil that she could no longer keep their secret. The first time she performed the title song from her album, she intended to tell the world that it was about Angelil.

Angelil finally gave in. One night in 1993, he treated Dion to a romantic candlelight dinner in their hotel room in Montreal. Dion recalled, "During the meal, he pulled a small box out of his pocket and put it on the table between us. He was nervous, intimidated too—it was very touching to see. 'I love you, Celine,' he told me. 'I love you like I've never loved anyone. I want to live with you.'. . .

Dion revealed her feelings for Angelil on her album The Color of My Love.

I opened the box and saw the engagement ring. I knew this meant that our love could finally be revealed."[95]

Dion has called November 8, 1993, "one of the best days of my life."[96] That day, *The Color of My Love* was released. The liner notes on the album included a dedication to Angelil, expressing Dion's love for him. Dion also spoke freely to the media and her fans that day, announcing her wonderful news.

Despite Angelil's fears that public reaction to their relationship would hurt her career, people generally responded positively to the news that the two planned to marry. "For once, René Angelil had been wrong," Dion wrote in her autobiography. "For years, he'd been afraid people would think we were wrong for each other and would accuse him of manipulating me. But just the opposite happened. There was an immensely sympathetic reaction, and not just for the moment. The public never doubted that we truly loved each other." [97]

Of course, some journalists and other people criticized the relationship between Dion and her much older manager. However, Dion did not care. "I don't read newspapers," she said. "I don't need to look at a newspaper to know who I am, what I like and what I don't like. I know what I did and what I didn't do, who I am, where I want to go, what I want to be. I love René. I think we're the perfect team." [98] She also said that "Love has no age." [99]

However, Dion and her family were upset when a Quebec tabloid, *Photo Police,* reported that Angelil and Dion had lived together before she was eighteen years old. This was a serious accusation, since, if it were true, Angelil could have been jailed. The couple, along with Dion's mother, sued the tabloid for $20 million. They eventually settled out of court, and the tabloid had to retract the story and make a donation to the Cystic Fibrosis Foundation of Quebec.

A Fairy-Tale Wedding

On December 17, 1994, Celine Dion and René Angelil were married at Notre Dame Cathedral in Montreal. The wedding was "like nothing ever before seen in Quebec. A very elegant, romantic dream." [100]

Thousands of fans lined the roads between the hotel and the cathedral. A carpet with "CR"—Dion and Angelil's initials—covered the street outside the church and ran up the aisle. Dion wore an elaborately decorated white dress with a long train, which was estimated to cost twenty-five thousand

In 1994 Dion and Angelil were married at Notre Dame Cathedral (pictured) in Montreal.

dollars. In addition, the ceremony was carried live on Canadian television and watched by millions of people.

The reception following the wedding was even more extravagant. The floor of the banquet room was covered with flower petals. Cages of cooing doves lined the room. Other rooms were decorated like a Parisian bistro, a Wild West saloon, a casino, an Arabian palace, and more.

Dion was criticized for her elaborate and expensive wedding. But she refused to feel guilty about her magical day.

> In Quebec, this event was talked about a lot, before, during, and after—and in every tone of voice. Certain people said I put too much into it, that I was making a display of my wealth, and that it seemed like a vulgar marketing event. But I'd been a little girl from Charlemagne who'd been kept from smiling at the world by two overlong teeth. I'd come a long way and gone far, carried by my voice, by the love of my family, by René, and by the Quebecois public. To show it and share it with others isn't publicity, it's gratitude.[101]

She also said, "I wanted to have a fairy-tale wedding—I was having a fairy-tale life!"[102]

Back to Work

After the wedding, Dion and Angelil had planned to take several months off for a honeymoon. However, they could not ignore

Obstacles to a Church Wedding

Dion and Angelil are Roman Catholic and were married in a Roman Catholic Church. At the time, their church wedding was the subject of some debate, since Angelil had been married and divorced twice before. The Roman Catholic Church does not recognize divorce, and it generally doesn't allow divorced people to marry in a Catholic Church.

However, Angelil was able to have his first marriage annulled. Annulment is a formal procedure by which the church acknowledges that the marriage was not valid because one or both of the participants was not mature enough to understand or fulfill the duties of marriage. When Angelil was married for the second time, it was in a civil ceremony, which is not recognized as establishing a Catholic marriage. Therefore, Angelil and Dion were able to have an official Roman Catholic ceremony for their marriage after they produced their baptismal certificates and had a meeting with a priest to determine the seriousness of their feelings for each other.

her career. Less than a month after the wedding, Dion was in London to do publicity for her new single, "Think Twice." She did not regret her decision, for, like Angelil, she loved to work. "I realized, a few weeks after my wedding, that I had become as ambitious as he, if not more. I had no real desire to stop working. Both of us wanted to go farther, higher. It was a fascinating journey. The road was beautiful and the scenery magnificent." [103]

Chapter 5

Singing for the Movies—and the World

THE 1990s WOULD see Dion become a major star in the United States and Europe. Dion would also become part of movie history when she recorded an unforgettable love song that touched millions of people around the world.

Movie Magic

Nineteen ninety-two was the year Celine Dion really broke through in America. Her album *Celine Dion* became her first gold record in the United States, and its single, "If You Asked Me To," held the number one spot on the charts for three weeks.

That same year, Dion recorded a duet with the singer Peabo Bryson for the Disney movie *Beauty and the Beast*. The title song became a Top 10 hit and was nominated for an Academy Award, or Oscar, for Best Song. Dion and Bryson were invited to sing the song at the Oscar ceremony in Los Angeles.

Singing at the Oscars gave Dion an unexpected attack of stage fright. The performance would be broadcast live to a television audience of more than a billion people. Dion was also awed by the stars in the audience. "Elizabeth Taylor and Paul Newman, Tom Cruise, Michael Douglas, Barbra Streisand, and Liza Minelli. Here were all the idols I'd always dreamed of meeting. Now I was seeing them at my feet, and I was singing for them. Now they were watching and listening to me, just as I'd always watched and listened to them." [104]

Angelil reminded Dion that "all these people are impressed by you as much as you could be by them,"[105] but Dion did not quite believe it. "I didn't yet completely see myself as a real star, equal to those around me,"[106] she reflected. Despite her insecurities, the performance went off without a hitch, and "Beauty and the Beast" won the Oscar for Best Song. The song also won a Grammy Award.

"Beauty and the Beast" was a turning point in Dion's career. Music journalist Chuck Taylor said that "'Beauty and the Beast' came along, and I think that was really the breakout song."[107]

"Beauty and the Beast" was the first time Dion was featured on a movie soundtrack, but it certainly was not the last. Her powerful voice and romantic style were soon in great demand for other films. "When I Fall in Love" from Dion's 1993 album, *The Color of My Love,* was the theme song for the hit romantic comedy *Sleepless in Seattle,* starring Tom Hanks and Meg Ryan. The song's popularity helped the album sell 11 million copies. But that was nothing compared with the movie and the hit song that still lay in Dion's future.

The Academy Awards

The Academy Awards are the highest honor given by the motion picture industry. They are awarded every spring by the Academy of Motion Picture Arts and Sciences for excellence in movie creation and production. Awards are given in a variety of categories, including Best Picture, Best Actor and Actress, Best Screenplay, Best Original Song, and technical categories such as Sound Editing, Art Direction, Costume Design, and Makeup.

In most categories, no more than five entrants are nominated by academy members who work in that field. For example, Best Director nominees are chosen by other directors. All members of the academy vote for Best Picture nominees. Then the winners are chosen by secret ballot. Special awards, honorary awards, and lifetime achievement awards are also presented.

The Academy Awards are also known as the Oscars, because a member of the film industry said the statuette given out as a prize looked like her uncle Oscar. The first Academy Awards were presented at a dinner in 1929. Today, the Academy Awards are given out at an elaborate ceremony that is seen by a billion television viewers around the world.

Meg Ryan and Tom Hanks's characters finally meet in a scene from Sleepless in Seattle. *Dion's "When I Fall in Love" is the theme song for the film.*

Along with recording albums and adding her talents to movie soundtracks, Dion also made many noteworthy public appearances in the early 1990s. She was honored to be invited to sing at the White House for President Bill Clinton. Dion also made many appearances on popular television shows, such as *The Tonight Show* and *The David Letterman Show*.

Returning to Her Roots

Although Dion was achieving phenomenal success as an English-language artist, she continued to record in French. In 1995, the only album Dion released was *D'Eux* (The title means "Two," although the spelling does not follow standard Parisian French.) It sold 5 million copies and became the best-selling French-language album in history, remaining at the top of the French charts for an astonishing forty-four weeks.

Canadian music journalist Alan Niester wrote that Dion "seems to have two careers"[108] because she recorded in two languages and promoted her albums in two very different markets. However, Dion did not see it that way. "I don't really consider it two different careers, more I consider it one full career. I do the French albums because it's in my blood and it's my origins and it's my roots. It is a must for me to sing in French in my life. Don't forget I started to sing in French. I have 11 French albums."[109] It was always important to Dion to stay true to her French-speaking Quebec roots.

New Heights

Dion reached new heights in 1996 when her album *Falling into You* became the biggest selling album of the year. It reached the top of the charts in eleven countries. Dion won music awards all over the globe, including the World Music Awards, the Juno Awards, and the Grammy Awards.

One of the reasons for *Falling into You*'s success was the song "Because You Loved Me," which was featured in the film *Up Close and Personal,* starring Michelle Pfeiffer and Robert Redford. The

The Grammy Awards

Every year in the United States, the National Academy of Recording Arts and Sciences (NARAS) presents Grammy Awards for excellence in the recording industry. Various types of music are featured, including rock, jazz, country, gospel, and classical. Grammies are also awarded for spoken-word recordings, children's music, music videos, television and movie soundtracks, and technical categories such as musical arrangement, engineering, and production.

NARAS was founded in 1957 and began giving out Grammy Awards in 1958. The award gets its name from an early record player called the gramophone, and the statuette is shaped like a gramophone. NARAS members, which include creative and technical professionals in the music industry, select the finalists and the winners. Special awards, including the Lifetime Achievement Award and the Grammy Legends Award, are also given to honor people who have made substantial contributions to the music industry over the years.

Although the Grammies have often been accused of being out of touch with modern music and current recording artists, the awards remain the biggest event of the music industry. In recent years, NARAS has tried to update its image by creating new categories to recognize popular music styles such as heavy metal and rap.

Dion promotes her album Falling into You *at a press conference in Montreal.*

single was number one in the United States for six straight weeks. "Because You Loved Me" was heard in every television commercial for the movie. Diane Warren, who wrote the song, thinks that featuring the song in the commercial helped make it a number one hit, and also helped make Dion so popular in the United States. "That's once-in-a-lifetime exposure for an artist,"[110] she said.

Even music critics, who sometimes dismissed Dion's vocal style as overemotional, complimented *Falling into You. Billboard* magazine called it "a deep album that will solidify Dion's reputation as one of the world's true pop divas."[111] Another trade paper, *RPM* magazine, said, "There's really not much need for criticism, because it would be fruitless. This album will sell a ton, and with a voice like that, she deserves every penny."[112]

Dion's tremendous success meant even more work for the singer. At one point, she was rehearsing to sing at several award shows, preparing her next English-language album, filming videos and television appearances, and traveling around the country to do interviews, promotional appearances, and a fund-raiser for the Canadian Cystic Fibrosis Foundation. Although she was exhausted, Dion found new confidence in herself. She was more willing to speak up when something was not going right, or to make her opinions heard in the recording studio or on tour. "René was still in control and still decided when to up the ante, but he listened to me more and more. David [Foster] did as well. And so did the people at Sony. I was becoming a mature and autonomous artist."[113]

In 1996, Dion sang before her largest audience ever. She was invited to perform "The Power of the Dream" at the opening

A giant puppet emerges from billowing sheets at the opening ceremonies of the 1996 Summer Olympic Games. Dion performed "The Power of the Dream" in front of her largest audience ever.

ceremonies of the Summer Olympic Games in Atlanta, Georgia. The song had been specially written for the Olympics.

As usual before a big performance, Dion was nervous. "It's like a leap into the unknown," she said. "And the more people and eyes and cameras there are, the greater and more terrifying this unknown becomes."[114] Dion's fears were not eased when her sixty-nine-year-old mother told her she was too nervous to attend the event and would watch her on television instead. However, Dion handled the performance with her usual flair and confidence, and dazzled the audience of eighty-five thousand spectators and more than 4 billion television viewers around the world.

Dion faced another huge television audience when she performed two songs at the 1997 Academy Awards. At first, Dion was only scheduled to perform "Because You Loved Me." Then, shortly before the ceremony, singer Natalie Cole, who was supposed to sing "I Finally Found Someone" from Barbra Streisand's movie *The Mirror Has Two Faces,* fell ill and had to cancel. The night before the show, Dion was asked if she could fill in for Cole. Although being asked to perform was a great honor, it also meant that Dion had to appear before a huge audience without much preparation. Many stars would not take this risk for fear of embarrassing themselves in public. Dion, however, quickly agreed to perform the song. Her only request was to have the lyrics written on a piece of paper and taped to her microphone stand, since she did not have time to learn the words of the song.

Journalists and music industry executives were impressed by Dion's confidence in performing a song she barely knew at such short notice in front of an audience that numbered in the billions around the world. "She didn't have to do that," said *Billboard* editor, Larry LeBlanc. "Some people wouldn't put themselves on the line like that. . . . A lot of artists would not want to have . . . set themselves up for failure."[115]

A Titanic Success

Shortly after the Academy Awards, a composer named James Horner approached Dion and Angelil and told them he was writing the music for *Titanic,* a movie directed by James Cameron, one of Hollywood's hottest directors. Horner had written a love song called "My Heart Will Go On" for the end of the film. There was just one problem: Cameron did not want a pop song in his movie. But Horner was sure that if he heard Dion sing his song, the director would change his mind.

Dion knew the song was right for her the first time she heard it. "He [Horner] explained the movie so well to me. I had tears in my eyes. I went to sing the song before I had seen the movie. I felt so strong and emotional that I was ready to go into the studio and sing."[116] She and Angelil agreed that Dion would record a demo tape of the song for Cameron to listen to. During the taping, people cried in the studio, they were so moved by Dion's voice and the power of the song.

Horner's plan worked. When Cameron heard the tape of Dion singing "My Heart Will Go On," he knew the song was just right for his film because it captured the emotions of the main character so

Kate Winslet (left) and Leonardo DiCaprio take direction from James Cameron (right) before filming a scene for Titanic. *Dion sang the theme song for the film.*

The *Titanic* Disaster

On April 14, 1912, the British luxury liner *Titanic* struck an iceberg in the North Atlantic and sank. More than fifteen hundred people died in one of the worst maritime disasters in history.

The *Titanic* was the largest and most elegant ship of her time. She was making her first voyage from Southampton, England, to New York City when she sank. The ship was considered unsinkable because it had sixteen watertight compartments. Engineers were confident that several of the compartments could fill with water without causing the ship to sink. However, the iceberg damaged so many compartments that the ship filled with water in a matter of hours.

Many of the passengers who died on the *Titanic* were poor immigrants traveling to America in third class. However, well-known, extremely wealthy, first-class passengers such as John Jacob Astor IV, Benjamin Guggenheim, and Isidor Straus (a founder of Macy's department store) also died. These upper-class people were the celebrities of their day, and the world was shocked and saddened at their loss of life.

The *Titanic* has been the subject of countless books, as well as several major motion pictures. The 1997 movie *Titanic* became the most popular motion picture of all time, as it combined romance and special effects to create an unforgettable and heart-wrenching story of true love and survival.

well. The song was also released as a single. Dion recalled that "everyone was so pleased with the demo we'd recorded . . . that we never went back to the studio to rerecord the song. That demo would go out around the world and would become . . . the best-selling song in the entire history of records."[117]

Titanic went on to become the most successful film of all time, holding the number one spot for fifteen weeks and earning more than $1 billion. "My Heart Will Go On" was a record breaker as well. The single entered the charts at number one and remained there for weeks. It was featured on two hit albums, the *Titanic* soundtrack and Dion's latest album, *Let's Talk About Love*. Together, those two albums sold more than 65 million copies worldwide.

Chuck Taylor of *Billboard* magazine called "My Heart Will Go On" "the ultimate ballad of the decade. It helped define the biggest movie in history."[118] *Entertainment Weekly* magazine called Dion "the voice that launched fifteen million albums."[119]

"Who knew what impact it would have on people?" Dion later said of the song which had become so incredibly popular. "You have a very strong love story to make people cry, and to make them want to hear the song and see the film three, four, and five times. It's a magic moment, and I'm glad they thought about me. I'm very proud that we said yes to it." [120]

In 1998, Dion made her third appearance onstage at the Academy Awards. She sang "My Heart Will Go On," then watched the song win Best Original Song. That was just one of the eleven awards *Titanic* won in its triumphant Oscar appearance.

Once again, Dion had made music history. Her career was at its peak. Then a medical emergency made Dion change her priorities. Suddenly, her career was not the most important thing in her life.

Chapter 6

Taking Time for Family

In March 1999, Dion was in the middle of a world tour. On a plane ride from Minneapolis to Dallas, Texas, Dion noticed Angelil rubbing his neck. She touched her husband's neck and felt a hard lump just under his right ear. Dion knew right away something was seriously wrong. She insisted that Angelil see a doctor as soon as they got to Dallas.

"Never in my life will I forget that terrible moment when a young doctor came to meet with us in René's room,"[121] Dion recalled in her autobiography. Their worst fears had come true: Angelil had cancer.

Coping with Cancer

At first, Dion was in denial that such a terrible thing could happen to them. She later said her first thoughts about cancer were, "That's for the others. I'm in show business. . . . But when it hits you, it changes your life forever. It changed René's life. It changed mine."[122]

Angelil immediately had surgery to remove the tumor. The operation was followed by thirty-eight chemotherapy and radiation treatments to eliminate any traces of cancer that the operation had missed. Dion wanted to cancel her tour, but Angelil refused to let her. "It's especially important that you don't stop," he told her. "It won't change anything, as you well know."[123] Dion agreed, but she did cancel some performances so that she could be at Angelil's side for every one of his treatments.

Angelil credits Dion's presence and dedication to helping him successfully battle the cancer. The experience also showed Angelil a new side of their relationship. "I used to be in love with her more than anything, but now there's not a word that exists that defines how much I love her."[124]

For her part, Dion just knew that Angelil needed her, as she had needed him for so many years. "He said to me that he needed me, and I felt so good," she recalled. "I felt that I could not only love him but I felt that I could make a difference in his life, and that's why I'm there."[125]

Targeting Cancer Cells

Many patients with cancer have surgery to remove malignant tumors. Although a large concentration of cancer cells (such as a tumor) can be removed surgically, cancer cells that have spread into the bloodstream and traveled to other parts of the body cannot be eliminated by surgery. Therefore, chemotherapy and radiation are also used to fight cancer. These treatments can be used after surgery, or before surgery to shrink a tumor so it can be operated on. They are also used to treat cancers that cannot be helped by surgery, such as leukemia (a cancer of the blood).

Chemotherapy is the name for more than fifty different anticancer drugs that interfere with a cell's ability to divide and grow bigger. Patients often receive a combination of more than one chemotherapy drug. The drugs are usually administered by injection directly into the bloodstream, or taken by mouth. Patients usually undergo several weeks of chemotherapy.

Because chemotherapy drugs cannot tell the difference between cancer cells and normal cells, these treatments affect all parts of the body and can produce severe side effects. Some of the most common include diarrhea, nausea and vomiting, hair loss, and anemia (low iron in the blood). Most of these side effects go away or are reversed after treatment is completed.

Radiation is often prescribed as a cancer treatment. Radiation treatment uses high-energy particles, such as X rays and gamma rays, to create genetic damage that destroys cancer cells. Because radiation can be focused specifically on tumors, there are fewer side effects than with chemotherapy. However, patients undergoing radiation treatments often suffer from extreme fatigue, loss of appetite, and skin damage at the site of the treatment.

In 1999 Angelil was diagnosed with cancer. Dion cancelled several concert dates to be with him during his treatment.

Dion also realized that Angelil's medical crisis had not been all bad. In her autobiography, she wrote, "I believe that in every misfortune there is good. René's illness brought us closer together. It changed our priorities and our dreams. I don't know what might have become of us if René hadn't gotten sick, but I think that it's definitely helped us gain depth and maturity in our relationship."[126]

Time for a Break

Although Angelil's cancer went into remission and he regained his health, the experience had shown the couple that Dion's career was not the most important thing in their lives. For years, the couple had talked about taking a break, but they had always let work commitments get in the way. Now, they decided to make that dream a reality. "We've had a message sent to us, so we're going to stop this show-business life,"[127] Dion explained in a television interview.

Dion wanted to make her last concert as special as possible, so she chose one of the most special nights—December 31, 1999, the end of the millennium. She would perform the concert in Montreal, where she had gotten her start so many years before. For Dion, it was an exceptional evening. "Each of the songs I did that night took on a new dimension. We were living the end of a dream, the end of the century. It was both heartrending and marvelous."[128]

As soon as the show in Montreal was over, Dion, her parents, Angelil, and a few friends flew to Las Vegas. There, she and Angelil renewed their wedding vows in another elaborate ceremony on January 5. Then the couple headed to their new home in Jupiter, Florida. It was time to start a new chapter in their lives.

Angelil and Dion renew their wedding vows in an elaborate ceremony in Las Vegas.

The Dions at Home

Since the age of twelve, Dion's life had been one of constant pressure. If she was not on tour, she was in the recording studio, making television appearances, or meeting record company executives and other important people in the music industry. Now, for the first time, Dion had time to relax.

In the early 1990s, Dion and Angelil had bought a home in West Palm Beach, Florida. Later, they paid $750,000 for land in Jupiter, a small island twenty miles north of Palm Beach, and built

Two Very Different Houses

Celine Dion grew up in a small, old-fashioned house. The first floor of the house had her parents' bedroom, a large living room, and a small sitting room, which was used only when important people came to visit. A narrow porch ran along the front of the house, with steps leading to the busy street in front. Like many old-fashioned houses, the kitchen was in a separate building attached to the house. The second floor had four crowded bedrooms. Dion and her sisters shared two of the bedrooms, while her brothers shared the other two.

During the mid-1990s, Dion began planning a dream house for herself and her husband in Jupiter, Florida. Dion spent weeks collecting photographs and articles from decorating magazines. She also made notes on what she liked and did not like about the objects in each picture. Dion's taste runs toward the romantic style, which is heavily decorated and comforting. Then Dion gave her ideas to a team of decorators, who drew up plans for the house. Dion and Angelil had already bought a lot in a gated community in Jupiter.

On July 28, 1998, the couple moved into their dream house. It is very different from the simple house where Dion grew up in Canada. This house has an inner courtyard filled with statues and plants. There are nine bedrooms, a dressmaking studio for Dion's mother and aunt to use when they visit, and numerous dining rooms, living rooms, and gourmet kitchens. All the rooms look out on an immense patio that is filled with different styles of gardens and an in-ground swimming pool with the couple's intertwined initials on the bottom. Finally, the house has thirty-three televisions and a large movie theater.

a large house in an exclusive gated community where several other celebrities have homes. Although Dion loved Quebec, she was so famous that she could not go out in public there without being mobbed by thousands of fans. The Dions needed a place that could be a private retreat, and they found it in Jupiter.

Although she thrives on stress and excitement, Dion soon found that she liked living quietly at home, too. "The things I really enjoy, maybe more than anything else, are cooking at my house and cleaning the house," she said. "I do! I do! I love cleaning. When I'm home, I do it myself and it relaxes me. . . . There's a lot more pressure in [the music] business and I just feel that I've stopped turning around. I'm going forward now." [129] Dion and her husband also spend a lot of time on the golf course, and Dion makes frequent shopping trips to expensive stores. Her passion for buying shoes has been widely reported in the press. "Celine has to buy shoes," says Angelil. "She cannot pass in front of a boutique and see shoes without going in and buying. . . . She has over 600 pairs of shoes at the house, it's unbelievable. She has shoes that she never wears. She just likes buying shoes." [130]

Baby Makes Three

For many years, Dion and Angelil had dreamed of having a child together. However, Dion's constant touring made this impractical. The hectic schedules and the stress on Dion's body were demanding even for a woman as young as Dion, and would not have been good for a developing fetus. In addition, the frequent separations from Angelil would have been especially painful and stressful for Dion if she were pregnant.

Angelil's cancer treatments also seemed to doom the couple's efforts to have a baby. The chemotherapy he had undergone had left him unable to father a child. However, before he started the treatments, he had had some of his sperm frozen and stored in a sperm bank. "It was obviously not the most romantic experience a couple could dream of," Dion commented. "But it gave us the confidence that, whatever happens, our dearest dream was possible." [131]

Babies from a Test Tube

In vitro fertilization, or IVF, has enabled couples who have been unable to have children to fulfill the dream of becoming parents. Because conception occurs in a laboratory, children conceived through IVF are sometimes called "test-tube babies."

Early in the IVF process, a woman takes hormones for several weeks to stimulate her ovaries to produce eggs. Then a number of eggs are surgically removed from the woman's ovaries and fertilized with sperm in a laboratory. A few days later, embryos have formed, and some of these are reimplanted in the woman's body, with the hope that at least one of them will develop into a baby. The success rate of IVF is between 20 and 30 percent. Some women must undergo more than one IVF treatment before becoming pregnant. Often, eggs or embryos remaining after a successful IVF treatment are frozen and stored for the couple to use later to have another child.

The first successful IVF pregnancy in humans occurred in 1978, when Louise Brown was born in England. Brown's birth caused a sensation, and she was featured in magazines and newspaper articles around the world. Since then, hundreds of thousands of babies have been born through IVF, and the procedure is considered a routine part of infertility treatment.

Once Dion had performed her final concert, she and Angelil could devote all their energy to seeking pregnancy. In May 2000, Dion underwent in vitro fertilization (IVF). A few weeks later, her doctors stopped by Dion's house in Jupiter with some fantastic news. Dion was pregnant!

The couple wasted no time sharing the news with their families and friends. However, unlike most couples, they also had to share the news with the media and the public. Within twenty-four hours, Dion's office issued a press release announcing her pregnancy. Dion did not mind the lack of privacy. "Our happiness had to be known. For twenty years we'd shared a kind of intimacy with the public at large. I wanted them to share our joy just as they'd shared our suffering. I believe you should never hide your happiness. It lights up and cheers up the world. To keep it only for yourself is to lose it."[132]

Dion and Angelil smile proudly after the baptism of their son, René-Charles.

Dion also wanted to get the news out before a tabloid printed an untrue story about her. In January 2000, she and Angelil had sued the *National Enquirer* for printing an incorrect story that she was pregnant with twins. Since she was not pregnant at that time, Dion said the story caused her "significant emotional distress." [133]

Dion's pregnancy was uneventful. On January 25, 2001, three weeks before her due date, Dion gave birth to a healthy son. The baby was named René-Charles. Dion called her mother while she was in labor, and Thérèse happily reported that "I heard the baby's first cry live on the telephone." [134]

Dion and Angelil were thrilled to be parents and settled into their roles with enthusiasm. Friends were not surprised at their joy. "This was their dream," record producer David Foster said. "It's bigger than any hit record, bigger than anything for them." [135]

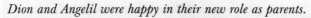

Dion and Angelil were happy in their new role as parents.

What Does the Future Hold?

Celine Dion has always believed dreams can come true, and she has been intensely dedicated to achieving her goals, both professional and personal. Her focus on her family led to many changes in her life, and she is not likely to go back to her old life of constant touring and recording any time soon. Dion took 2001 off to be with her son. However, she did perform "God Bless America" at the star-studded *America: A Tribute to Heroes* telethon to raise money for the survivors of the devastating terrorist attacks of September 11. Dion plans to take most, if not all, of 2002 off as well.

Dion and Angelil also hope to have more children. During the multistep IVF procedure that led to her pregnancy with René-Charles, at least one other embryo was frozen for later implantation. In an interview on Canadian television in December 2000, Dion made it clear that she intends to try to achieve another pregnancy. "I will go get it [the embryo]. That's for sure."[136]

Although she is focused on her family, Dion loves being onstage too much to give up performing completely. In 2003, she will begin a long-term engagement in Las Vegas, performing two hundred nights a year at the Colosseum. This schedule will allow Dion to spend time with her family and avoid the constant traveling of a concert tour.

In an interview on VH1, Dion said of her personal life, "Go for this life too. It's important that you have it."[137]

The Secrets of Her Success

Throughout her career, Dion has been the subject of thousands of news stories. Like any celebrity, some of these stories have been negative, but in general, Dion's image is extremely positive, and she is viewed as a dedicated professional and a genuinely nice person. Part of this positive opinion can be attributed to her close ties with René Angelil, who has taken great steps to protect and control her image ever since she was a child. But a more important reason is Dion's own personality and dedication.

Many superstars have reputations as being difficult or demanding, but the musicians and producers who have worked with Dion over the years have praised her positive attitude and dedication to recording and performing the best music possible. Journalists, too, have found Dion to be easy to get along with. "You'll very rarely see bad press on her," says *Billboard* editor Larry LeBlanc, who has written extensively about Dion and Angelil over the years. "A part of it also is she is not afraid of making fun of herself, when she's gone over the top. The way you see her on stage is the way she is." [138]

LeBlanc recalls being invited backstage with his son, Robin, after one of Dion's Canadian shows. After talking for several minutes, LeBlanc prepared to leave, since many other people were waiting to meet the singer. Instead, Dion "said, 'no, no, no.' And kept us there for ten more minutes. It was a genuine interest." Even more surprisingly, LeBlanc said, "When I ran into her six months later at a party in Quebec City, she turned to me: 'How's Robin?'. . . Most of these people don't remember your name when they leave you, never mind what your kid's name is a few months later." [139]

Dion performs at a concert in Montreal. She is known for her dedication and hard work.

Dion enthusiastically signs autographs for some adoring fans.

Dion also has a genuine affection for her fans and has spent a great deal of time signing autographs, visiting schools, and talking to young people about her career and her life. Unlike many superstars, it seems that she is always willing to make time for the public. *Entertainment Weekly* reporter Jeff Gordanier recalls Dion's performance at the 1997 Blockbuster Awards in Los Angeles. Although the singer was clearly exhausted at the end of the show, she signed autographs for about fifty fans lined up outside the theater. "She signs books, records, pads, hands, the sleeve of someone's red silk shirt. . . . Then she does something that divas—even burgeoning ones—aren't supposed to do: She searches the crowd for more." [140]

Another writer, Richard Crouse, recalls Dion rolling down the window of her limousine to wave at fans after a concert in Montreal because she was afraid the crowd would not be able to see her through the tinted glass. Early in the singer's career,

Dion has always been thankful for her success.

Angelil's second wife, Anne, told Dion that "a smile is worth a million dollars," and that smiling "will make your fans happy."[141] Dion is happy to comply, and, Crouse reports, "To this day it is rare to see her in public without a beaming smile, looking lovingly at her fans."[142]

Dion also finds strength in her family. She is still close to her parents and siblings and has been very generous to them. She bought her parents two houses, one near Montreal and another in the Laurentian Mountains. She has also given her parents large sums of money and expensive gifts. Dion has given $100,000 to each of her brothers and sisters, and regularly pays for Christmas shopping trips for her thirty-two nieces and nephews. In return, Dion relies on her family to keep her grounded and happy, and spends a great deal of time with them. She even talks with her mother every day on the phone. "She doesn't forget who she is. That's what impresses me the most,"[143] says Angelil.

Dion's incredible determination and love have brought her to a level of stardom few entertainers have reached. Throughout her life, Dion has single-mindedly pursued her dreams. Behind her ambitions is one simple fact: She loves to sing. "I hope to sing for the rest of my life, because I really am sincerely happy to be able to do it," she told an interviewer early in her career. "I don't want a hit. I want a career."[144] Celine Dion has had all that and more.

Notes

Chapter 1: A Musical Childhood

1. Quoted in Richard Crouse, *A Voice and a Dream: The Celine Dion Story.* New York: Ballantine Books, 1998, p. 5.
2. Celine Dion, *My Story, My Dream.* New York: HarperCollins, 2000, p. 21.
3. Dion, *My Story, My Dream,* p. 22.
4. Quoted in Jeremy Dean, *Celine Dion: Let's Talk About Love.* New York: Welcome Rain, 1998, p. 11.
5. Quoted in Dean, *Celine Dion: Let's Talk About Love,* p. 14.
6. Dion, *My Story, My Dream,* p. 23.
7. Dion, *My Story, My Dream,* p. 32.
8. Dion, *My Story, My Dream,* p. 20.
9. Quoted in Crouse, *A Voice and a Dream,* p. 9.
10. Dion, *My Story, My Dream,* p. 38.
11. Quoted in Crouse, *A Voice and a Dream,* p. 11.
12. Dion, *My Story, My Dream,* p. 28.
13. Dion, *My Story, My Dream,* p. 34.
14. Quoted in Dean, *Celine Dion: Let's Talk About Love,* p. 12.
15. Quoted in Barry Grills, *Celine Dion: Falling into You.* Ontario, Canada: Quarry Music Books, 1997, p. 32.
16. Dion, *My Story, My Dream,* pp. 37–38.
17. Dion, *My Story, My Dream,* p. 77.
18. Quoted in Grills, *Celine Dion: Falling into You,* p. 51.
19. Quoted in Dean, *Celine Dion: Let's Talk About Love,* p. 15.
20. Dion, *My Story, My Dream,* p. 48.
21. Dion, *My Story, My Dream,* p. 51.
22. Quoted in Dion, *My Story, My Dream,* p. 51.
23. Quoted in Dion, *My Story, My Dream,* pp. 51–52.
24. Dion, *My Story, My Dream,* p. 56.
25. Quoted in Dean, *Celine Dion: Let's Talk About Love,* p. 17.
26. Dion, *My Story, My Dream,* p. 56.

Chapter 2: Taking the Challenge

27. Quoted in Grills, *Celine Dion: Falling into You,* p. 43.

28. Quoted in Dion, *My Story, My Dream,* p. 58.

29. Dion, *My Story, My Dream,* p. 59.

30. Quoted in Crouse, *A Voice and a Dream,* p. 22.

31. Quoted in Grills, *Celine Dion: Falling into You,* pp. 43–44.

32. Quoted in Dion, *My Story, My Dream,* p. 63.

33. Dion, *My Story, My Dream,* pp. 64–65.

34. Dion, *My Story, My Dream,* p. 111.

35. Dion, *My Story, My Dream,* p. 75.

36. Quoted in Crouse, *A Voice and a Dream,* p. 24.

37. Quoted in Grills, *Celine Dion: Falling into You,* p. 26.

38. Quoted in Crouse, *A Voice and a Dream,* p. 27.

39. Quoted in Grills, *Celine Dion: Falling into You,* p. 46.

40. Quoted in Grills, *Celine Dion: Falling into You,* p. 46.

41. Quoted in Crouse, *A Voice and a Dream,* p. 30.

42. Dion, *My Story, My Dream,* p. 76.

43. Quoted in Dean, *Celine Dion: Let's Talk About Love,* p. 20.

44. Dion, *My Story, My Dream,* p. 77.

45. Dion, *My Story, My Dream,* p. 82.

46. Quoted in Dion, *My Story, My Dream,* pp. 65–66.

47. Quoted in Grills, *Celine Dion: Falling into You,* p. 14.

48. Dion, *My Story, My Dream,* p. 113.

49. Quoted in Grills, *Celine Dion: Falling into You,* p. 46.

50. Quoted in Dion, *My Story, My Dream,* p. 79.

51. Dion, *My Story, My Dream,* p. 86.

52. Dion, *My Story, My Dream,* p. 86.

53. Dion, *My Story, My Dream,* pp. 87–88.

54. Dion, *My Story, My Dream,* p. 95.

55. Dion, *My Story, My Dream,* p. 96.

56. Dion, *My Story, My Dream,* p. 97.

57. Dion, *My Story, My Dream,* pp. 102–103.

58. Quoted in Crouse, *A Voice and a Dream,* p. 30.

Chapter 3: Conquering America

59. Quoted in Crouse, *A Voice and a Dream,* pp. 36–37.

60. Quoted in Grills, *Celine Dion: Falling into You,* p. 51.

61. E!Online interview, www.eonline.com/Celebs/Qa/Dion/interview 3.html.

62. Quoted in Grills, *Celine Dion: Falling into You,* p. 68.

63. Quoted in Dean, *Celine Dion: Let's Talk About Love,* p. 21.

64. Quoted in Crouse, *A Voice and a Dream,* p. 37.

65. Quoted in Crouse, *A Voice and a Dream,* p. 38.

66. Quoted in Crouse, *A Voice and a Dream,* p. 40.

67. Quoted in *Behind the Music: Celine Dion,* VH1, 2000.

68. Quoted in *Behind the Music: Celine Dion,* VH1.

69. Quoted in *Behind the Music: Celine Dion,* VH1.

70. Quoted in Grills, *Celine Dion: Falling into You,* p. 48.

71. Quoted in *Behind the Music: Celine Dion,* VH1.

72. Quoted in Grills, *Celine Dion: Falling into You,* p. 63.

73. Quoted in Grills, *Celine Dion: Falling into You,* p. 63.

74. Quoted in Crouse, *A Voice and a Dream,* p. 35.

75. Quoted in Grills, *Celine Dion: Falling into You,* p. 27.

76. Quoted in Crouse, *A Voice and a Dream,* p. 48.

77. Quoted in Crouse, *A Voice and a Dream,* pp. 48–49.

78. Quoted in Grills, *Celine Dion: Falling into You,* pp. 70–71.

79. Dion, *My Story, My Dream,* p. 178.

80. Quoted in Grills, *Celine Dion: Falling into You,* p. 79.

Chapter 4: True Love—and Heartache

81. Dion, *My Story, My Dream,* p. 104.

82. Dion, *My Story, My Dream,* p. 104.

83. Dion, *My Story, My Dream,* p. 105.

84. Dion, *My Story, My Dream,* pp. 123–24.

85. Dion, *My Story, My Dream,* p. 133.

86. Dion, *My Story, My Dream,* p. 133.

87. Dion, *My Story, My Dream,* p. 155.

88. Dion, *My Story, My Dream,* p. 159.

89. Dion, *My Story, My Dream,* p. 169.

90. E!Online interview, www.eonline.com/Celebs/Qa/Dion/interview 3.html.

91. Quoted in Crouse, *A Voice and a Dream,* p. 76.

92. Quoted in Crouse, *A Voice and a Dream,* pp. 76–77.

93. Dion, *My Story, My Dream,* p. 218.

94. Quoted in *Behind the Music: Celine Dion*, VH1.

95. Dion, *My Story, My Dream*, p. 212.

96. Dion, *My Story, My Dream*, p. 218.

97. Dion, *My Story, My Dream*, p. 221.

98. E!Online interview, www.eonline.com/Celebs/Qa/Dion/interview 3.html.

99. Quoted in *Behind the Music: Celine Dion*, VH1.

100. Dion, *My Story, My Dream*, p. 231.

101. Dion, *My Story, My Dream*, p. 232.

102. Quoted in Dean, *Celine Dion: Let's Talk About Love*, p. 38.

103. Dion, *My Story, My Dream*, p. 233.

Chapter 5: Singing for the Movies—and the World

104. Dion, *My Story, My Dream*, p. 197.

105. Dion, *My Story, My Dream*, p. 197.

106. Dion, *My Story, My Dream*, p. 198.

107. Quoted in Grills, *Celine Dion: Falling into You,* p. 158.

108. Quoted in Grills, *Celine Dion: Falling into You,* p. 158.

109. Quoted in *Behind the Music: Celine Dion*, VH1.

110. Quoted in Crouse, *A Voice and a Dream*, p. 106.

111. Quoted in Crouse, *A Voice and a Dream*, p. 109.

112. Quoted in Crouse, *A Voice and a Dream*, p. 109.

113. Dion, *My Story, My Dream*, p. 237.

114. Dion, *My Story, My Dream*, p. 241.

115. Quoted in Grills, *Celine Dion: Falling into You,* p. 16.

116. Quoted in Dean, *Celine Dion: Let's Talk About Love,* p. 61.

117. Dion, *My Story, My Dream*, p. 260.

118. Quoted in *Behind the Music: Celine Dion*, VH1.

119. Quoted in Crouse, *A Voice and a Dream*, p. 153.

120. Quoted in Crouse, *A Voice and a Dream*, p. 140.

Chapter 6: Taking Time for Family

121. Dion, *My Story, My Dream*, p. 270.

122. Quoted in *Behind the Music: Celine Dion*, VH1.

123. Quoted in Dion, *My Story, My Dream*, p. 273.

124. Quoted in *Behind the Music: Celine Dion*, VH1.

125. Quoted in *Behind the Music: Celine Dion*, VH1.

126. Dion, *My Story, My Dream*, p. 289.

127. Quoted in *Behind the Music: Celine Dion*, VH1.

128. Dion, *My Story, My Dream*, p. 290.

129. Quoted in Grills, *Celine Dion: Falling into You*, p. 162.

130. Quoted in Grills, *Celine Dion: Falling into You*, p. 162.

131. Dion, *My Story, My Dream*, p. 9.

132. Dion, *My Story, My Dream*, p. 16.

133. Quoted in Jill Smolowe, "Expecting the Best," *People Weekly*, June 26, 2000, pp. 50–51.

134. Quoted in Anne-Marie O'Neill, "Boy Oh Boy!" *People Weekly*, February 12, 2001, p. 93.

135. Quoted in O'Neill, "Boy Oh Boy!" p. 94.

136. Quoted in O'Neill, "Boy Oh Boy!" p. 98.

137. Quoted in *Behind the Music: Celine Dion*, VH1.

138. Quoted in Grills, *Celine Dion: Falling into You*, p. 89.

139. Quoted in Grills, *Celine Dion: Falling into You*, p. 150.

140. Quoted in Grills, *Celine Dion: Falling into You*, p. 176.

141. Quoted in Crouse, *A Voice and a Dream*, p. 23.

142. Crouse, *A Voice and a Dream*, p. 23.

143. Quoted in Crouse, *A Voice and a Dream*, p. 32.

144. Quoted in Grills, *Celine Dion: Falling into You*, p. 177.

Important Dates in the Life of Celine Dion

1968

Celine Dion is born to Adhemar and Thérèse Dion in Charlemagne, Quebec, Canada.

1973

Dion makes her first public performance singing at her brother's wedding.

1980

Dion records two songs written by her mother and brother, and sends the tape to manager René Angelil.

1981

Dion releases her first two albums, *La voix du bon dieu* and *Celine chante Noël,* and becomes a huge star in Quebec.

1982

Dion wins two awards at the Yamaha World Song Festival in Tokyo, Japan.

1986

Dion takes a year and a half off to learn English and change her image from child star to adult performer.

1987

Dion releases *Incognito,* an album that successfully shows her new sound and image.

1988

Dion wins the Eurovision song contest in Dublin, Ireland.

1990

Dion's first English-language album, *Unison,* is released, and Dion becomes popular in the United States.

1992

Dion records "Beauty and the Beast" with Peabo Bryson for the soundtrack of the Disney movie.

1993

Dion and her manager, René Angelil, reveal their romantic relationship.

1994

Dion and Angelil are married on December 17.

1997

Dion records "My Heart Will Go On" for the movie *Titanic.*

1999

Angelil is diagnosed with cancer. Later that year, Dion performs her last concert and leaves show business to spend time with her husband.

2001

Dion gives birth to a son, René-Charles.

For Further Reading

Books

Biography Today, 1997 Annual Cumulation, "Celine Dion," 1997. Provides an overview of Dion's life and career, along with a list of her CDs, honors and awards, and addresses where fans can contact the star.

Melanie Cole, *Celine Dion.* Childs, MD: Mitchell Lane, 1999. An interesting and easy-to-read look at Dion's life and career.

Norma Jean Lutz, *Celine Dion.* Philadelphia: Chelsea House, 2001. An in-depth look at Dion's personal and professional lives.

Websites

Celine Dion (www.celineonline.com). The official website for Dion; includes information, message boards, and chat.

E!Online (www.eonline.com). Type "Celine Dion" into the search box at this E!Online website to access an interview and many news items about the star.

Passion Celine Dion (www.celine-dion.net). Includes lyrics for all of Dion's songs, translated into English and other languages.

People.com (www.people.aol.com). Click on "People Profiles," then type in Dion's name. You can also access past *People Weekly* magazine articles on the star from this website.

Sony Music (www.sonymusic.com/artists). The website of Dion's record company includes information about her CDs.

Works Consulted

Books

Richard Crouse, *A Voice and a Dream: The Celine Dion Story*. New York: Ballantine Books, 1998. A behind-the-scenes look at Dion's life, written by one of Canada's top music journalists.

Jeremy Dean, *Celine Dion: Let's Talk About Love*. New York: Welcome Rain, 1998. A well-written book about Dion's career and background.

Celine Dion, *My Story, My Dream*. New York: HarperCollins, 2000. A detailed look at Dion's life and career, written by the star herself.

Barry Grills, *Celine Dion: Falling into You*. Ontario, Canada: Quarry Music Books, 1997. This detailed look at Dion's career includes a lot of information about the music business and how it works.

Periodicals

Celine Dion, "The Pursuit of Happiness," *People Weekly,* October 23, 2000.

Anne-Marie O'Neill, "Boy Oh Boy!" *People Weekly,* February 12, 2001.

Jill Smolowe, "Expecting the Best," *People Weekly,* June 26, 2000.

TV Broadcast

Behind the Music: Celine Dion, VH1, 2000. This one-hour program focuses on Dion's life and career, and includes on-camera interviews with her, as well as other members of the music business.

Index

Picture Credits

About the Author

Joanne Mattern is the author of more than one hundred nonfiction and fiction books for children. Her favorite subjects are animals and nature, but she has also written biographies of explorers and sports figures, an encyclopedia on American immigration, classic novel retellings, and activity books. Ms. Mattern lives in New York State with her husband and young daughter.